The 8 Keys to Becoming Wildly Successful and Happy

By: Harry A. Olson, Ph.D.

i

The 8 Keys to Becoming Wildly Successful and Happy

Library of Congress Cataloging in Publication Data

Published by:

Insight Publishing Company
P.O. Box 4189
Sevierville, TN 37864
Printed in USA

Cover Design by: Alan Lyle

ISBN No. 1-885640-41-2

Prologue

Success without happiness is hollow.
Happiness without success is self-deception.

Truly, you can't have one without the other.

It is a sad commentary on modern life that far too many people go to their grave with their music still inside them.

This needn't be **your** fate.

Success **and** happiness are your **birthright.**

This book gives you a **new system** for channeling your intelligence, talents and skills to help you claim and fulfill that birthright, and to give you the extra edge you deserve.

Congratulations as you set forth upon the greatest adventure life has to offer!

> "Success is doing something so well that they'd pay you to do it, and love to do it so much that you'd do it for free."
> Cavett Robert

Harry A. Olson
Baltimore 1998

The 8 Keys to Becoming Wildly Successful and Happy

This book is dedicated to

Two of the people I most admire -
my wife, Carol,
and
my son, David
who in several important ways are examples
of true achievement and
who sincerely make a difference.

My parents, Axel and Mary,
who taught me from the beginning
the necessary skills and values
to live a victorious life.

Terry Wright - a true survivor
whose grit and faith are an inspiration
to all who know her.

ACKNOWLEDGMENTS

First of all, a large debt of gratitude goes to my wife, Carol, for her faith in me and her assistance with manuscript preparation.

I wish to deeply thank the following friends and colleagues:

David Wright, my publisher, who over the years has given me his ongoing interest, support and advice.
Stevan Meizlish, who taught me the value of "selling the postage stamp", and helped me devise the current format for The 8 Keys books.

Rick Ottenstein, Stacy Shamberger, Wally Brown, Richard Schimberg, Michael Teitelbaum, Gordon Shea, Mike Goodrich, Bob Kalinoski, Judy Pressman, Sheryl Stephenson, A. Lynne Puckett, Burton Linne, my friends in the Pikesville 3 Chapter of Business Network International, who all provided support, encouragement, and direct and indirect input to this project,

and

My coaching and counseling clients who really taught me most of what I know about success and happiness.

Table of Contents

Introduction   xi
Building inner power and resilience:
The 8 Keys Model is and how it works
How to use this book   xxv

Chapter One
What it Takes to Succeed and be
Happy in the Next Millennium   1

Chapter Two
High-Jump or Limbo: What Do You
Do With the Bar?   6

Chapter Three
What is the Secret of Your Greatness?   18

Chapter Four
Redefining Competing and Winning   27

Chapter Five
Key 1 - Basic Goal
"Be Significant - Make a Difference"   41

Chapter Six
Implementing Key 1-Exercises   57

Introduction to Keys 2,3,4
Courage/Emotional Self-Reliance   63

Chapter Seven
Key 2 - Self-Definition
"Be Yourself - Be Ego Flexible"   67

Chapter Eight
Implementing Key 2 - Exercises   79

Chapter Nine
Key 3 - Center of Control
"Call Your Own Shots"   87

Chapter Ten
Implementing Key 3 - Exercises   101

Chapter Eleven
Key 4 - World View
"See Value and Opportunity Everywhere"   111

Chapter Twelve
Implementing Key 4 - Exercises   123

Introduction to Keys 5, 6, & 7
Energy/Action   133

Chapter Thirteen
    Key 5-Process
    "Streamline Your Energy"   135

Chapter Fourteen
    Implementing Key 5 - Exercises   153

Chapter Fifteen
    Key 6 - Focus
    "Keep Your Eye on The Ball"   163

Chapter Sixteen
    Implementing Key 6 - Exercises   179

Chapter Seventeen
    Key 7 - Meaning of Activity
    "Find Joy in The Journey"   189

Chapter Eighteen
    Implementing Key 7 - Exercises   201

Introduction to Key 8
    Expansion/Outreach   209

Chapter Ninteen
    Key 8 - Relationships
    "Empower Yourself Through
    Empowering Others"   211

Chapter Twenty
    Implementing Key 8 - Exercises   225

Epilogue   235

Appendix 1   How to Create Affirmations and
              Visualizations   237

Appendix 2   List of Feelings that Persons
              Have but Often Fail to Identify   241

Appendix 3   Igniter Phrases   244

Appendix 4   Shame-Sham   246

Additional Resources   251

References   253

About the Author   257

"The significant problems we face cannot be solved with the same level of thinking we were at when we created them."

Einstein

The power to be your best,
to solidify your career,
or to transform an organization,
is directly distributed within
8 Key Dimensions.
How you act in these areas
makes all the difference.....

H.A.Olson

INTRODUCTION

Building Inner Power and Resilience: What The 8 Keys Model is and how it works

The 8 Keys unlock the door to a **vibrant, successful and happy way of life**, joyous and liberating. This model will open new vistas and enable you to be all that you can be . . . and then some . . . in both your career and your personal life.

The 8 Keys Model has identified the **essential qualities** that produce peak achievement and fulfillment. It gives you a coordinated **system**, a step-by-step process, to help you maximize your potential in your own way. As you take each step, success builds upon success.

The 8 Keys Model is so powerful, because it is so basic and universal. It gets to the core of what empowers ordinary people to do extraordinary things. It also strengthens "emotional intelligence" (EQ), emotional/behavioral control and flexibility. As such, The 8 Keys serve as a compatible **foundation** for other positive self-improvement or corporate teamwork and organizational development initiatives. **Success with The 8 Keys promotes faster and stronger results with these other approaches as well.**

The 8 Keys model goes far beyond old motivational strategies and hype. It cuts to the core of the very way we perceive and think about success. It completely reinvents competition and winning from the ground up, cutting out the destructive parts and building on positive strength. It streamlines energy and reduces stress and struggle.

Is the "New Model" really new? Yes and no. The foundations lie in the wisdom of the ages, so often overlooked today. Built on these foundations is the latest scientific research on what **really works** in the areas of competition and peak performance, as well as almost a quarter of a century of personal experience and insights from coaching and working with hundreds of top achievers in business, sales and athletics, and with corporate culture transformation in both large and small firms.

In development since the early 80's, I first introduced this model in 1990 in **THE NEW WAY TO COMPETE**. Since then my challenge has been to "operationalize" it, to make it simple to understand and implement. This Handbook presents a stepwise progression of the model, coupled with methods that you can apply at each step to tie principle to action, to drive new learning home.

THE POWER OF A MODEL

Many self-help and motivational books provide great techniques, yet most people don't follow-up on them or use them to their fullest. Part of the reason is that independent "techniques" are usually uncoordinated. It's like trying to cook a soufflé with a little of this and a little of that, **without a recipe**. To do that is to court failure. People soon quit.

A model coordinates techniques and ties them back to principles. A model says "That's why you're doing this, and here's how this fits into the overall scheme of things." Techniques are like the branches of a tree; the leaves are the results of their use. What would happen to the branches, what chance would the leaves have, if there were no trunk? The model is the trunk. It connects and ties the branches to a solid foundation which provides the life support of understanding, meaning and truth.

THE CORE OF THE SYSTEM

The 8 Keys are eight specific powerful **behavioral qualities** which differentiate healthy competitors and achievers from those who burn out, act destructively, or fold under pressure. These qualities impact how people interpret and act upon their experience and thus set themselves up for success or failure. **Growth in these qualities significantly alters hidden patterns and self-fulfilling prophecy**, both for individuals and organizations.

These qualities make natural sense and are easy to understand. They can be learned and developed by anyone.

DESCRIPTION: THE 8 KEYS MODEL

There are **eight critical broad dimensions** to the task of competing and achieving increasingly consistent peak performance. Distraction or major misdirection of energy in any one of these dimensions can undermine your strength and effectiveness, while champion individuals and organizations have it more together in these areas. These dimensions are

Basic Goal -What is the ultimate purpose of your actions. All behavior is goal-directed, serving a purpose, whether you are consciously aware of that purpose or not.

Self-Definition - How do you view yourself and your capabilities.

Center of Control - Who determines your feelings and actions: you, others, or circumstances.

Worldview - Your image of the world: how it operates, and your place in it.

Process - How you go about doing what you do, achieving your goals.

Focus - Where, and toward what, do you place your attention and energy for best results.

Meaning of Activity - Where do you get your payoffs from your actions, internal and external motivation.

Relationships - What do others mean to you and how do you work with them to accomplish goals.

The power to be your best, to solidify your career and to transform an organization is directly distributed within these dimensions. How you act in these areas makes all the difference. The 8 Keys Model helps you break the process of traditional win-lose, beat-the-opponent competing and achieving out into component attitudes and actions according to these eight dimensions, and then spells out a whole new method for "healthy competing" and achieving within the same framework. (See Box 1) Such a breakdown is essential to discovering how to escape the traps of destructive cultural programming and to selecting appropriate alternatives.

The right column outlines the eight liberating qualities which parallel those in the traditional model, listed in the left column. The eight attitudes and qualities in each column are arranged in an order that flows, each one overlapping and implying the one above and below it. A **shift** occurs at each horizontal rung as you move away from the attitude and behavioral quality on the left, embracing and developing the one on the right. As you make each shift, you strengthen and develop the positive behavioral qualities of true championship.

There is an important reason why the model is presented in this way. On the path of positive self and organizational development, it is as critical to know what to avoid as it is to know where you're headed. **You need to know what to release as well as what to embrace**. Spelling out the model in terms of dichotomy and contrast makes choices more clear.

THE 8 KEYS
Traditional vs New Model of Competing

Eight behavioral-cognitive shifts are required to create and maintain the new paradigm of positive competition and peak performance.

CURRENT WIN-LOSE MODEL COMPETING IN TODAY'S SOCIETY	THE 8 KEYS MODEL OF HEALTHY COMPETION COOPERATION & ACHIEVEMENT
(The 8 qualities below stem from and reinforce this model.)	(The 8 qualities below stem from and reinforce this model.)

FROM: TO:

1. GOAL:
   Striving for Superiority   →→→→→→   Striving for Significance
2. SELF-DEFINITION
   Self-protective   →→→→→→   Self-confident
3. CENTER OF CONTROL:
   External   →→→→→→   Internal
4. WORLD VIEW
   Scarcity   →→→→→→   Abundance
5. PROCESS
   Struggle   →→→→→→   Flow
6. FOCUS
   "How I'm Doing"   →→→→→→   "What I'm Doing"
7. MEANING
   Outcome Satisfaction   →→→→→→   Process Satisfaction
8. RELATIONSHIPS
   Winning Over Others   →→→→→→   Winning Through Others

ULTIMATE SHIFT
   Fear   →→→→→→   Faith and Trust

CORE ISSUES IN THE 8 KEYS

The basic issues involved in The 8 Keys also flow in a sequential, developmental manner.

Key 1 is the Foundation Key: setting a new course, determining your purpose.

Keys 2, 3 and 4 are the Courage/Emotional Self-Reliance Keys: Personal - letting go of ego traps, fears of success or failure, and self-defeating patterns, building confidence. Social - getting unhooked from comparison, envy, anger, etc., taking your power back within yourself. Attitudinal - building optimism, creativity, and expanding your horizons.

Keys 5, 6 and 7 are the Energy/Action Keys: How do you maximize your energy? Where and how do you direct your energy for best results? Where and how do you get your main motivation and pay-offs?

Key 8 is the Expansion/Outreach Key: How do you fully value and connect with others to achieve goals?

As you make progress on any one Key, you make developing the subsequent Keys easier.

THE 8 KEY GUIDELINES

Each of the eight shifts has a key guideline for growth that can be spelled out as an overriding maxim or principle. There is tremendous power, and some paradox and subtlety, involved in each shift. Therefore The 8 Key Guidelines do not capture all the meaning in each key, but they crystallize the central intent and direction. Here they are:

1. Be significant - make a difference
2. Be yourself - be ego flexible
3. Call you own shots
4. See value and opportunity everywhere
5. Streamline your energy
6. Keep your eye on the ball
7. Find joy in the journey
8. Empower yourself by empowering others

As you examine the diagram, notice the arrow from the bottom of the chart leading back to the top. The path to true winning isn't linear. Our metaphors of cause and effect and the "upward climb" are all flawed in this regard. The diagram is an abstraction. In real life the true interactions of The 8 Keys are much more circular, web-like, fluid and integrated.

Notice the "ultimate shift" at the bottom of the diagram. **There are only two major cognitive-emotional-spiritual forces in life: fear and faith. Faith pushes and pulls us forward, while fear pushes and pulls us back. Individual and collective human progress stands in the vortex of the force-field created by the perceived balance of fear and faith.** Our task, then, is to increase the power and experience of faith and trust, while reducing the hold of fear. In this model, "faith" and "trust" are action verbs, not just nouns. Faith and trust are what you do, not just what you have.

Faith breeds love, hope, calm, confidence, courage and commitment. As you succeed at each step on the path you strengthen your faith and trust in yourself, in others, and in an overriding sense of ultimate purpose in life. If you have religious faith you will find that area strengthened as well, although this model is silent on religious issues.

Faith and trust are reciprocal in The 8 Keys. Practicing The 8 Keys principles and skills strengthens faith and trust, which in turn strengthens you and your ability to implement the new model. Bottom line - you get stronger.

The core of the traditional model is fear. Fear, shame and discouragement are the basic motivations which drive negative cutthroat competition and lie at the root of most difficulties in achieving teamwork in organizations: fear of loss of status, admiration, position, income, etc. Fear impairs our ability to concentrate, recall and plan effectively. Fear increases distrust, anger and the risk of error, and impedes performance. The old model leads to subtle self-sabotage.

Born out of fear, the operational metaphor for the old model is struggle . . . struggle with opponents, struggle to win, struggle with oneself. Struggle spells stress and that is precisely what traditional competition produces in spades. (See Box 2 at the end of this chapter.)Born out of and strengthened by faith and trust, the operational metaphor for the new model is **artistry**. Artistry spells freedom, flexibility and flow.

THE ARTIST-WORKER

Artist athletes and workers are one with their craft. They love what they do. They experience an arousal that gets them positively psyched for the contest or the job, and which provides the mental and physical energy needed for peak performance. While they work intensely, work takes on the quality of play and/or artistic craftsmanship. Concentration and focus are enhanced. Productivity and contribution arc increased. Efforts are streamlined. Burnout ceases to be an issue. The new model increases one's sense of purpose and meaning in life and work, which in turn promotes confidence and reduces stress, anxiety, phobias, depression and other emotional and stress-related physical disorders. **The 8 Keys promote the self-reliance, resilience, collaboration and interdependence required today to succeed.**

xxi

THE NUGGETS

This Handbook gives you the nuggets, the necessary core concepts and actions you need to succeed. It focuses on The 8 Key Guidelines (the right-hand column of Box 1), bypassing the "cognitive shift" aspects of the model and some of the finer subtleties, distinctions and details that require more time and space to explore.

If you find that you want more, the **Additional Resources Section** at the end of this Handbook lists follow-up items that will take you deeper and farther. The **Playbook** provides systematic exercises and activities, with a place to record your actions and results. It is a self-help companion to this Handbook.

BOX 2

PITFALLS IN THE EIGHT DIMENSIONS ENCOURAGED BY TRADITIONAL COMPETITION

1. BASIC GOAL, PURPOSE
   The traditional goal is "Beat the Opponent" which can turn into a warfare mentality and "win at all costs." This can compromise ethics and values, and lead to destructive behaviors. Win-lose competition is an external goal and motivator because the outcome involves the actions of both yourself and others. Desire to win can eclipse desire to excel.

2. SELF-DEFINITION
   Our self-image, self-worth, and egos quickly get wrapped up in whether we win or lose and where we stand relative to others. We can become very self-protective or defensive. Losing can become internalized, causing bitterness and lowering of self-esteem. Losing can trigger shame. To the degree this occurs, we may limit our contributions and/or undercut others.

3. CENTER OF CONTROL
   Opponents readily become the "ones to beat." This inadvertently makes others our standard bearer and object of comparison. Anger, excessive comparisons, envy, jealousy and "keeping up with the Joneses" behaviors readily develop, robbing us of inner peace.

4. WORLD-VIEW
   Highly competitive people tend to believe "the best things in life are scarce." This encourages pessimism or guarded optimism and excessive personal worry and unrest. Enmity easily develops when people compete for things they fear they cannot share. It reduces big-picture thinking and the search for new or broader opportunities.

5. PROCESS
   Highly traditionally competitive people view life and success as a struggle-with opponents and with themselves. Thus energy is wasted and goal-directed effort is diluted.

6. FOCUS
   Focus often centers on how one is doing relative to others, as opposed to the goal and task at hand. Worrying about relative standing while you're actually competing or performing can cause you to make unnecessary mistakes. Traditional competing can divert attention and energy into tripping up opponents rather than minding one's own business.

7. MEANING
   Many highly competitive folks postpone gratification and enjoyment of practice and preparation until they know whether they've won or lost. If they lose, they can get discouraged and feel that all their preparation energy was wasted Internal motivation is diminished.

8. RELATIONSHIPS
   Traditional competition promotes division, power jockeying, suspicion, inequality, and occasionally anger. When the goal is to win. Others must be defeated by definition. Equality and sharing cannot co-exist with a competitive attitude.

The more the competitive mind set spills over into everyday life and work, the greater the power of these pitfalls to distort and impair key attitudes, actions and relationships.

HOW TO USE THIS BOOK

Make this book your personal catalyst or coach. It will support and challenge you, and point out certain steps and directions. Do the book, don't just skim it. Read with a purpose. The following tips will help:

- Specifically apply each of The 8 Keys to your personal situation, needs and goals.

- With every chapter and Key issue, ask:
  What does this mean to me?
  Where am I strong?
  What areas do I need to develop?
  What resources can I use?
  What obstacles/fears must I overcome?

- Don't dismiss an issue in which you're already well developed. That area is a power-source for you. Find ways to fine-hone those skills to make them even better.

- Over 100 "exercises" are presented. Some of these are consciousness-raisers or skill builders. Many go beyond "technique". They are peak performance practices that will help you develop habits of success. Daily apply the ones that are most applicable to you. Use them as is or adapt them as you see fit.

- Mental Training Exercises (visualizations, affirmations) are included for each Key. They are a vital and fun component in speeding your growth. Do them as is, or adapt them, but practice them daily. See Appendix 1 for tips in developing and using these.

- Set targets. Create and follow a **written action plan** to keep yourself on track. Make a contract with yourself to accomplish the plan. Using the Playbook will also help.

Growth only comes from within, not from outside. You need to take charge of your learning, or else little will happen. There are no shortcuts to success, but the 8 Keys identify attitudes, skills, and practices that will get you farther, faster and easier.

You may have even faster success and more satisfaction if you team up with a family member, friend, or coworker to work through the 8 Keys together. Consider taking an 8 Keys training course. Use the book in the way that best meets your needs. If you need to, **give your self permission to release your full capability and forge your own destiny.**

The 4 "Ds" of Success

Desire
Dedication
Determination
Discipline

"The next millennium requires a whole new pioneering spirit, comprised of self-reliance and interdependence."

H.A. Olson

To succeed, you have to *prepare* to succeed.

John Avianantos

**"Change is our constant partner.
We need to dance with it joyfully."**

H.A.Olson

**"Regardless of your profession,
YOU are the only real tool you've got.
Keep it fine-honed, ever sharp, ever ready."**

H.A.Olson

Chapter One

WHAT IT TAKES TO SUCCEED AND BE HAPPY IN THE NEXT MILLENNIUM

We didn't just go through a "recession" a few years ago. What really happened is that as we are closing this millennium, we are closing our current chapter of human history. We are at a turning point in time. We stand at the threshold of a new era. Within one generation, the systems we have been putting in place for the last 400 years - in business, education, government and in society at large - have become antiquated, passé, and in some measure irrelevant.

We are entering a thrilling new renaissance. The future will belong to renaissance children, women and men. This is the most exciting time to be alive, and also perhaps the scariest.

We experience a fractured world. The institutions, even many of the ideas and rules, that we've come to rely on, appear to be crumbling around our feet. Change is hurtling along at warp speed, causing shock waves at all levels in society. It will never slow down. Will we have what it takes to ride the wave, or will we get swamped and drowned by it?

THE NEW REALITY

In spite of a growing economy, and virtually unlimited opportunity, a pervasive sense of fear and helplessness pervades our society. No wonder.

Somehow we sense a vital truth that few people have openly identified: **the new demands we now face require new roles and sets of skills that are diametrically opposed to the ones in which we've been trained**. The methods that have made us great in the past can sink us in the future.

Managers were trained to be bosses. Now they're supposed to be coaches, facilitators, empowerers. Workers (and students) were trained to do as they were told. Now they need to be always-learning, creative problem solvers. Today, "teamwork" is in. When I went to school, teamwork was relegated to the playing field. In class, it was called "cheating". The new demands, and the roles they have created, caught us off guard, unprepared, with little or no time to catch up.

Here's the bottom line. The guarantees are going, going, gone. The motto of the brave new world is "if it's to be, it's up to me." Never before in human history have individuals had to take so much personal responsibility for their lives, with so little help from society's institutions, from business and government, all the way down to the family.

3

Whatever your career or future goals, today we all need to be **self-starting, self-motivated, self-directed and self-controlled, and self-responsible.** Not just having excellent skills, we must also be **emotionally self-reliant**, able to take pressure in stride and bounce back when buffeted.

At the same time we also must learn to be **interdependent**. Beyond being able to cooperate and collaborate, we must stand ready and able to forge lasting, mutually contributory and beneficial relationships. Managing our emotions and developing our interpersonal skills is becoming increasingly critical to achieving success.

TOMORROW'S WORLD

With the breakdown of large corporations which threw like-assigned people together willy-nilly, "virtual organizations" and **networks** will dominate the business and social world of tomorrow. They will at once be narrow and global - and hence more selective. "Community" will no longer be just geographically defined. Truly **who** you know may count as much as **what** you know. It is from out of our networks that tomorrow's greatest opportunities will arise. Information and ideas will dominate. Standards are stiffer. "Excellence" is no longer the ceiling. It's the floor. It's your admission ticket for the right to join the players.

Thus, the "rugged individualist" pioneer goes the way of the dinosaur. Tomorrow's pioneers forge into

4

uncharted systems, creating new models, methods and opportunities as they go - doing so hand in hand with others. Together we will write the next chapter, and fashion and shape our brave new world.

All of this takes **resilience**. This little handbook gives you a systematic way to strengthen yourself, to build confidence, to meet the challenges, to create and capitalize upon opportunity - to **forge your destiny** - and **to have a lot of fun and satisfaction** in the process.

It's going to be an exciting, wild ride. Let's get rolling!

"Above all else, the greatest predictor of your success and happiness is your vision for your future."

H.A. Olson

"Life's most important games are won or lost in the mind, before the game ever begins."

H.A. Olson

"You are not your job. You are your dreams and visions."

David Sandler

"Hold a picture of yourself long and steady enough in your minds eye, and you will be drawn toward it."
(You will become it.)

Harry Emerson Fosdick

"Next to the power of love, the greatest force in the world is the power of expectation."

H.A. Olson

Chapter Two

HIGH-JUMP OR LIMBO:WHAT DO YOU DO WITH THE BAR?

With high jump, you set the bar and jump over it. You keep raising the bar until it's so high that you knock it off its pegs when you jump at your highest level. With diligent practice, you could jump higher and raise the bar another notch.

In limbo, you waddle under the bar. After each pass-under, you lower the bar. You keep lowering the bar until you touch it going under, or you fall on your butt.

THE KEY TO YOUR SUCCESS

The key to your success and happiness boils down to this: **what are you doing with the bar?** Are you playing high-jump or limbo?

The "bar" is the outer limit of your perceived capability, as defined by your self-image. It is your subjective sense of your boundary, the ceiling above which you don't believe you can rise. It is your **self-expectation level**.

Try this exercise right now, before reading further. Stand up straight, raise your right arm vertically **as high as you possibly can**. (Stretch)

Now stretch an extra quarter inch.

Could you do it? If so, then when you stretched your arm initially, it **wasn't** as high as you **possibly** could, even though you thought it was.

This exercise demonstrates a vital truth:

MOST OF THE LIMITS WE EXPERIENCE ARE NOT DEFINED BY OUR CAPACITY, BUT BY OUR PERCEPTION AND EXPECTATIONS.

Sometimes our perceived limits are consciously defined. Years ago, no one believed that it was physically possible for a human being to run the mile in less than four minutes. No one had ever done it. That's why no one had ever done it! Then Roger Bannister accomplished it. The next season, several other runners did it. The season after that, several hundred runners did it. Roger Bannister didn't just break a record, he shattered a prevailing mindset limit. Usually **it's not ignorance that holds us back, but WHAT WE THINK WE KNOW.**

More often, however, the limits we apply in our daily lives are subconsciously determined. We aren't consciously aware of them on an ongoing basis, but we act

8

according to them anyway. When certain opportunities or challenges come our way and we shrink back, make excuses, or in some other way avoid meeting them even though we want to, the probability is high that at some inner level, we don't think we have what it takes. We often assume, "I can't do that" before we even have explored what's involved.

Years ago, Seattle Slew was touted as the greatest racehorse of all time. She blew her opponents away at the Kentucky Derby. So much so, in fact, that several of the horses that opposed her at the Derby were withdrawn from the Preakness.

At the Preakness, Seattle Slew exploded out of the starting gate, took an immediate 4-horse-length lead and kept that lead right through the finish. Afterward, Seattle Slew's jockey said "I didn't have to push that horse." When the times for all the races on Preakness Day were posted, it was noted that the 8th race, the one just before the Preakness, was run a split second **faster** than Seattle Slew's time! Why did the other jockeys in the Preakness let Seattle Slew keep such a lead? Could it be that they psyched themselves out, that they **didn't think** they could win, . . . or **expected** to lose? **Our outcomes are created by our expectations**.

PERFORMANCE ALWAYS MATCHES
SELF-IMAGE

If we think we have what it takes, or a reasonable chance to succeed, we're more likely to push the limits, take a risk - play high jump.

If we doubt ourselves, fear we might fail or be humiliated, we are more likely to shrink back, hem ourselves in, play it safe, even subconsciously sabotage our own efforts - play limbo. Pretty straightforward, isn't it? Here's how it works:

Your "self-image" is your inner picture of yourself. It is your belief-system about who and what you are, how strong or weak you are, how lovable and worthwhile you are, how superior or inferior you are in comparison to others, how good you look, and what you're capable of accomplishing in life. It's your "gut feeling" of what you've got going for or against you when you have to deal with life's challenges.

Every event, achievement, failure, encouragement, criticism and relationship in your life has helped to shape your self-image for better or worse. Your self-image is totally subjective. It's really a fiction, based on **your interpretations and reactions** to the experiences of your life. Yet even so, your self -image determines "you", your reality. It also determines and limits the course of your actions because humans always act **as if** what they believe to be true is actually so.

10

Your "self-esteem" is the **value** you place upon yourself, based on your self-image.

THE ROLE OF YOUR SUBCONSCIOUS

Your subconscious mind directs and controls your self-image. . . and your emotions, habits, physiology, and even what you see or don't see. Outside your conscious awareness, your subconscious orchestrates your mind and body in such a way that your performance level is always consistent with your self-image. It does that to protect you, to keep you from getting in over your head. Thus your subconscious creates self-fulfilling prophecy.

It sets the bar based upon what you imagine and tell yourself you can or can't do. Your subconscious can't distinguish between fantasy and reality, yet it works to **manifest into reality** whatever you consistently fantasize, expect, or believe about yourself. Therefore, behavior which is consistent with your self-image feels comfortable, right and natural for you. It's "habit". Behavior which is inconsistent feels more strange, awkward or risky.

When new behavior becomes better or more comfortable through practice, the subconscious has altered your self-image to incorporate it. If new behavior remains awkward, chances are that your self-image has resisted it.

Experiences of achievement, success, and encouragement can help to raise your bar. They help give

11

you the courage to try harder, to take more risks. Discouragement, fear, shame, humiliation, negative thinking and self-doubt can lead you to underestimate your capability and become more cautious and resistant to change, lowering your bar.

In short, if I can "see myself" performing in a new way, I will do so. If I can't see myself performing that way, I won't, and if I "try", I will soon quit and return to my old ways.

With self-image, **what you "see" is what you get.**

THE SECRET TO LASTING IMPROVEMENT

Suppose you want to change a habit, to grow, to try something new, perform at a new height. It doesn't matter if your goal is to win an Olympic medal, perform at your peak at work, or break free of the grip of fear or of an addiction. The ultimate task is the same.

The Key to making any new behavior last is to **change your self-image** to incorporate and be compatible with the new behaviors. You do this by **replacing self-limiting images and beliefs with self-liberating** ones. You can speed up this **process** by consistently visualizing yourself acting in the desired ways and telling yourself positive messages or affirmations that support the new image. When that happens, change will begin to take place automatically, without conscious effort. Bit by bit, you "find yourself" beginning to act according to your new self-image.

Unless self-image accepts it, the change will not last, no matter how hard you "try". Why? Part of you is trying, while another part of you doesn't believe it will happen, or expects to fail.

When Will and Imagination are in conflict, Imagination always wins. Will may try hard; Imagination sets the bar. What you "imagine" is guided by your self-image.

Let's take an example: trying to quit smoking. Admittedly, smoking is one of the toughest habits to kick. Yet if I truly believe I can do it, if I can **see myself** as a non-smoker, if I will incorporate "non-smoker" into my conscious and subconscious self-image, I will succeed. If I see myself as failing, if I don't think I'm "strong enough", I will ultimately fail, no matter how hard I try to quit - unless in the course of trying, my self-image changes.

That's also why fear can be so tough to eradicate. Once you become afraid you usually see yourself as less able to cope with the object of your fear. You give it more power over your life than it deserves, and deny power within yourself. If you avoid what you fear, you never get to find out what you can really accomplish. Fear is False Evidence Appearing Real. **The only way to eliminate fear is to reprogram your subconscious.**

You see, **we always live up- or down- to our expectations and beliefs about ourselves**. Performance always matches self-image. That's self-fulfilling prophecy.

Others also play a tremendous role in where our bar is set. If those around us encourage us, expect us to succeed, subconsciously we begin to feel stronger. If they discourage us, belittle us, or quietly expect us to fail, we can begin to lose faith in ourselves. How have the main people in your life impacted your success?

THE CONFIDENCE ZONE

For performance purposes, the subconscious mind creates and assumes a confidence level, or behavioral range consistent with our self-image, within which we routinely operate.

If we perform below our self-expectations, we will usually motivate ourselves to pull our performance up.

Sometimes, however, we "outperform" ourselves. If we exceed our expectations, we are operating out of our confidence zone at the upper end. The mind cannot tolerate inconsistency within the self-image for very long. Disparity between performance and self-image always causes discomfort and must be reconciled. Therefore, we must either raise the confidence zone (the bar) or lower the future performance.

This is where flexibility of the self-image comes in. Suppose a "B student" gets an A in a tough subject. If he says "Wow! I can do better than I thought. I must be good at this subject", he'll probably continue to get A's because he raised his perception of his ability (his bar, his self-image). He will see the possibility of "A" work as "natural" for him. What if he says "That A was nice, but it was a fluke. The teacher graded easy this time." What do you think he'll get on the next test? In this case he absorbed the A into his current "B student" self-concept, dismissing it and nullifying its impact.

Now here's the tricky part. If our "B student" is conscientious, he will "try his best" when he studies and prepares for his next test. He **wills** to get an A, but if he **imagines** himself as a "B student" in this subject, he will probably get a B. Why? Because of how he subconsciously sets the bar! He **thinks** he's preparing his hardest, but somehow he unwittingly might shoot himself in the foot either in preparation or at test time so that he just misses the mark. Then, if he gets a B on his next test, he can say to himself, "I guess I was right. I'm just a B student after all." How many of us sacrifice greater opportunity because we need to be "right" in our current assumptions?

Have you had any experiences like this?

PERFORMANCE AND GROWTH

The subconscious always plays limbo. From **its** perspective, you always perform at or under the bar.

Therefore, whenever there is an issue of increased performance, the task is to **raise the bar,** to expand the self-image to incorporate new behaviors. We need to bring Will and Imagination into line at a higher level.

HOW TO RAISE THE BAR

- Open yourself to new possibilities.
- Develop your confidence.
- **Expect** to succeed.
- Set very specific, reachable goals. Setting unrealistically high goals causes frustration and lowers self-image, possibly creating a self-fulfilling prophecy of failure.
- Consciously picture yourself successfully acting in new ways. The visualizations and affirmations in this book will help you immensely. (See Appendix I)
- Be diligent, and give it time. It takes 21-30 days to ingrain new habits of thought and action. Take it easy.
- Pace yourself reasonably. Inch by inch, anything's a cinch.

All of the above, and much more, will be spelled out and paced for you as you proceed through the 8 Keys System.

Now - **what are you doing with your bar?**

"To achieve greatness -
start where you are,
use what you have,
do what you can."

Arthur Ashe

"What you have is far less important
that what you <u>do</u> with what you have."

H.A. Olson

"Every person is a vast hidden treasure.
You discover the riches when you
care enough to look beneath the surface."

H.A. Olson

Chapter Three

WHAT IS THE SECRET OF YOUR GREATNESS?

If someone were to ask you that question for real, how would you respond? Would you be shocked? Would you say, "Who, me?" Would you feel uncomfortable, not having a ready answer?

Truth be told, the vast majority of us would say "yes" to these responses, if for no other reason than **no one** has probably **ever** asked you that question before.

I'm asking it now - to you - for real!

Most of us don't see ourselves as possessing "greatness". . . nor "genius", nor "creativity", nor "brilliance" Why?

Society has bamboozled us on this one. We have been conditioned to believe that only a very small percentage of the population possess these qualities to any great degree. The rest of us supposedly hover around "average".

"Average" is strictly a mathematical term. It is only the number you get when you add a column of figures and

19

divide by the number of figures in the column. That's it. Nothing more.

We have been taught to use the word "average" as a judging, comparative term, meaning "mediocre". That's OK, as long as it is **never applied to personal human qualities**. Apply it to my performance, perhaps; to my self, to my personhood - never!

Furthermore, society has also taught us to pay much more attention to our, and other's, mistakes than to our successes. The result? We all carry around a much heavier bag of inferiority feelings than necessary. Most of us could write a book about our weaknesses, but might have a hard time filling a postage stamp with our strengths. Many of us are embarrassed when our strengths are mentioned. A lot of folks have trouble accepting compliments and deny or negate them when they occur. The bottom line: **we sell ourselves short on the things that matter most**.

GREATNESS - YOUR BIRTHRIGHT

The human being was created for greatness. Look at the vast possibilities built into the human musculature and mind. The limits of greatness don't lie with our capabilities, but with society's definition.

We all have the potential for greatness - in skills, in mind, in deeds. All too often, however, our true greatness remains as potential rather than coming out in our daily activities. This is largely because we don't "see" ourselves

20

as "great people" in any more than a vague pat-on-the-back sense. When we do something great, we often dismiss it, or deny it, because our self-image says its not "natural" for us to be great.

We all have different, unique sets of skills, assets, talents, capabilities. It doesn't matter if the playing field is unequal, because the expression of our greatness isn't a competition.

Nor is greatness simply the "high end" of a particular quality. I will never forget attending the funeral of a friend's son many years ago. Our friends had six children. The oldest - the deceased - was mentally retarded. He never worked, nor lived outside the home. He was in many ways a drain on the family resources. Yet at the funeral, all of his siblings spoke of how he taught them the true meaning of love and caring. That was a life of greatness on the part of the deceased in a very special way.

We don't need to be celebrities, or nationally or locally acclaimed heroes to be great. We just need to believe in ourselves, to do our part, to do our best with the strengths and talents at our command, to play well the hand we have been dealt. First, however, we need to know what those strengths and talents are.

AN EXERCISE

On a separate piece of paper, list all of your strengths, assets, talents, capabilities that you can think of.

21

Brainstorm. Don't censor this list. Add to this list frequently. Note which of - and how - these strengths show up in your daily behavior, either in direct expression or behind the scenes (such as, you're using your creativity when you come up with a good idea on the job.) Also list specific adversities or limits you have coped with or overcome. Sometimes greatness comes from our strengths, and sometimes it comes as we rise to the occasion to meet positive or negative challenges. Sometimes it is born out of tragedy. Difficulties often teach us more imortant lessons than success does. St. Paul said, "Suffering produces endurance, and endurance produces character, and character produces hope." Pay particular attention to your adaptive strategies and overall character strengths which you used to cope with difficulties. Daily continue to collect all the "positive evidence" that you can.

The purpose of this exercise is twofold: First, to reopen your window on yourself, and raise your appreciation of yourself as a person of true greatness (not to swell your head nor to get you on an ego trip!)

Second, to provide a focus for your particular expression and outworking of your strengths and talents as you work and play through the 8 Keys. The 8 Keys will serve to liberate and channel your greatness.

This list will become a vital tool in your expansion of your success and happiness. Now for the exercise.

Get ready.....
Get set.....
GO!

Appreciate yourself for what you are and what you've done! . . . Right now, while you're in "process". You don't have to wait until you've made more money, lost more weight, etc., to accept yourself fully. You **can do so** now, even though you may have more you wish to accomplish.

How you describe yourself impacts your self-image. Following is a list of powerful descriptive adjectives that will help you identify a broader range of your greatness quality.

Once you have completed the list, take a few moments to relax, close your eyes and **visualize** yourself as a person of greatness. See yourself acting out your greatness qualities in some way, at work or in your family, or social life. See others benefitting from what you do or offer. Have fun!

POSITIVE DESCRIPTIVE ADJECTIVES

Adaptable
Affectionate
Ageless
Artistic
At Ease
Athletic
Attractive
Aware

Balance
Beautiful
Bright
Brilliant

Calm
Capable
Captivating
Caring
Centered
Challenging
Charismatic
Collected
Comfortable
Committed
Compassionate
Competent
Competitive
Confident
Conscientious
Control, in

Cool
Courageous
Creative

Dedicated
Delightful
Diligent
Demonstrative
Dutiful

Educated
Effective
Effervescent
Efficient
Elated
Electrifying
Empathic
Encouraged
Encouraging
Energized
Exciting
Ecstatic

Fascinating
Flexible
Focused
Forgiving

Generous
Genius

Gifted
Giving
Glib
Generous

Happy
Hard-working
Harmonious
Helpful
Humorous

Imaginative
Indestructible
Influential
Inspirational
Inspired
Insightful
Interesting
Invincible

Jocular
Just
Joyful

Kind

Knowledgeable

Lavish
Leader

24

Level-headed
Lovable
Lovely
Loving

Magnanimous
Magnetic
Marvelous
Methodical
Meaningful
Motivated
Motivating

Natural

Optimistic
Overcome

Passionate
Philosophical
Popular
Positive
Potent
Powerful
Purposeful

Quick
Quick-witted
Quiet

Religious
Righteous

Sensitive
Skilled
Smooth
Solid
Spirited
Spiritual
Strong
Successful

Talented
Tender
Timeless
Thoughtful

Vibrant
Vivacious
Vivid
Victorious
Visionary

Warm
Wealthy
Well-liked
Wholesale
Wholesome
Wise
Witty
Wonderful

Young at Heart
Zany

"We have confused purpose with process achieving with competing and success with victory."

H.A. Olson

"It's a fascinating form of insanity, the belief that by repeating the same acts one will now achieve different results."

H.A. Olson

Chapter Four

REDEFINING COMPETING AND WINNING

Down through the annals of time, there has been - and always will be - only one way to determine whether you win or lose. What do you think that way is?

Think about it. The answer is not as obvious as it might first appear.

A man in his early twenties decided to run in a major city marathon. He had no prior running experience. He was checked by his doctor and found to be fit. He hired a running coach to work with his feet, and he hired me to work with his head for quick peak performance. There was only one problem. He decided to be a runner when the marathon was only six weeks away.

By the fourth week he was running thirteen miles every other day. His feet, form, and head were all in gear. On the day of the marathon, he was psyched up and totally prepared. He ran his best.

The next week he burst through my office door yelling, "I won! I won!" Knowing who the marathon winners actually were, I asked, "Won what?" "The marathon!", he shouted, excited and out of breath. "Come

28

on", I told him, "Your performance was miraculous, but you didn't get a prize!" " Oh, I didn't **win**! I finished in the second thousand, but I finished without stopping or quitting. I didn't hit the 'wall' and I met my goal. That's what I meant when I said I won."

Now, do you know the answer to the opening question?

In the 1984 Olympics, a swimmer won the gold medal and set a world record, but when interviewed, he cried and was very bitter. The medal was meaningless, because he had a private goal which he didn't meet.

Now you know. **The only way to determine whether you win or lose is how you define winning and losing**. Winning and losing - and succeeding and failing - are totally subjective. They do not depend on the outcome of any particular contest. What counts for your self-definition as a "winner" or "loser" is not the actual final standing but how you **interpret** your performance.

YOUR LANGUAGE SHAPES YOUR OUTCOMES

Eliminate terms like "loser" and "failure" from your vocabulary. They have no place as descriptions for people. People may lose a contest, they may fail in their attempt at reaching a goal. That does not make them "losers" or "failures". Any win or loss, success or failure is only one pin-point in a life span. It is impossible - and very unfair - to class an entire person with all his or her complexity or potential on the basis of a specific performance. To label someone, yourself included, as a "loser" or "failure" can do severe harm to one's self concept, produce shame, and inhibit future performance.

THE FUNDAMENTAL MINDSET SHIFT

COMPETITIVE GOAL:
Strive for Superiority VS Strive for Significance

Winning traditionally means beating the opponent. Carry that to its ultimate conclusions and you have war! The goal is to be above others, to be superior in a comparative sense, to be the best. But winning in this sense is an external goal, dependent not only on what you do but also on the actions of your opponents. This puts the outcome out of your direct control. That's why people cheat - to increase their degree of control over the outcome. (The nature of traditional competition actually encourages cheating, by the way, in spite of our social lip service against it.) This lack of control over the final outcome initially may add to the fun and challenge. But as the stakes for winning and losing get higher, personal pressure and stress can mount to severe proportions.

WHICH GOAL WORKS BETTER?

How well does this goal of beating others motivate peak performance? Only up to a point. My friend and mentor, Dr. Lars-Eric Unestahl, headed up the Institute of Sport Psychology at Orebro University in Orebro, Sweden. In this position, and also privately, he provided mental training to thousands of professional and world-class amateur athletes over the years. Part of his program focused on goal definition, and here he found interesting results.

When an athlete first entered Unestahl's program, he or she was asked what his or her goals were. Usually the athlete would say, "To beat so-and-so in the next competition." The athlete then was asked to visualize that goal. What happened? His or her performance improved - for about two weeks or so, and then it plateaued. As the athlete learned to focus the goal away from beating others to a personal, noncompetitive performance standard, such as "running the mile in 3.5 minutes", performance improved even more, and continued to improve. Hundreds of others studies on competition in business, sports and academia have come to the same conclusion.

As these findings indicate, there is a bell-curve relationship between performance and competitive goals. Performance in the service of a competitive goal (beating someone else) will rise to a certain point. If the person concentrates too much on that goal, his or her performance will actually begin to worsen. Why this happens will be explained later when we discuss energy. It's better to shoot for a personal non-competitive goal.

The traditional competitor, then, in attempting to one-up others, is looking for elite status. His interest is in himself, often at the expense of the opponent. While you may be engaged in a "friendly" competition, the very nature of traditional competition puts you at odds with your opponent. After all, you're trying to beat him. You won't give him any advantage. Your behavior and his are negatively linked. If you help him, you hurt your own chances of winning. So much for "friendly competition". Down deep there really is no such thing.

Whenever the pressure to win eclipses the need to achieve, and beating the opponent becomes the primary objective, backstabbing, cheating or other immoral or illegal acts can easily escalate. What's worse is that these behaviors often become legitimized in the service of the overall objective ("the ends justify the means."). Thus unless we are very careful, goals and objectives can become confused and energy can get diverted from the real task into useless, often destructive channels.

We see this happening occasionally in sports. How much more can it occur in informal competition in the workplace or elsewhere, where the "rules" are unwritten and the "game" never ends?

STRIVING FOR SIGNIFICANCE

The 8 Keys Competitor, on the other hand, strives for **significance**. He or she realizes that achieving excellence is more important than winning. All you must do to win is to edge out the opponent. You don't necessarily have to be excellent to do that. Therefore, winning and excellence often pull in opposite directions.

In fact, people who focus primarily on winning will often stop when they think they've done enough to beat all comers. A second grader was reading books for a school read-a-thon. He quit after reading forty seven books because he figured he was way ahead, even though he had several weeks until the contest was over. On awards day he was shocked into tears because he didn't win. Someone else read sixty seven books! The story of "The Tortoise and the Hare" and the Seattle Slew experience in Chapter 2 have the same implication.

Of course, the 8 Keys Competitor wants to win and will work very hard and smart. But **how** he or she wins is of vital importance. His or her key emphasis is on achieving a standard of excellence, on being his or her personal best. This is an internal goal, unlike "winning". No other persons need to be involved in the goal. The Healthy Competitor recognizes a vital truth: **go for excellence, for achievement, make a lasting contribution, and the winning will take care of itself.**

This is profound, but traditional competitors will consider it naive. That's because they are unwilling or unable to **trust** this principle. They are so busy struggling that they undermine the full power of their resources. They accomplish what they do in spite of themselves, whereas the 8 Keys Competitor maximizes his or her potential in efficient channels.

Significance taps very deep, primal roots. It is human nature to want to excel, to achieve for achievement's sake. Think how many of us put great energy and meticulous attention into personal crafts, hobbies, projects, sports or goals, or overcome great obstacles without any notion of reward beyond the satisfaction of a job well done. Others may praise our efforts, but that is not the primary reason we do such things. The real drive comes from within, and at that level has nothing to do with beating others. In fact, these people usually deny competitive motives or speak of "competing with myself".

When you focus on the standard you wish to achieve for yourself rather than a position relative to others, the whole ball game changes. Your actions become more "streamlined". Stress level drops, you worry less, it's easier to concentrate. Energy is more easily liberated and channeled in the most efficient way. This frees you to perform even better because your energy is focused on the task at hand, not upon your opponents, nor the final outcome. This is the experience of the artist-athlete, being one with his performance.

Kristi Yamaguchi put it so well after winning the Gold in Women's Figure Skating at the '92 Olympics. "Sometimes I wonder why I compete. But I never wonder why I skate. When I'm out there on the ice, my goal is to give the audience the very best performance I'm capable of giving."

This is a basic distinction: the traditional competitor focuses on **getting**, perhaps the Gold Medal, the prize, the glory or maximizing profit. The True Champion focuses first on **giving and performing**, and knowing and trusting that what goes around comes around. (See Box 4.1 at the end of this chapter.)

You can "win" every time you play, as long as your definition of winning isn't tied solely to the score. Let your definition include lessons learned, friends made, new experiences, etc.

Focus on being **your** best. It's the only way you'll get a shot at being **the** best.

MENTALLY SOFT VS MENTALLY HARDY

Research by psychologists Suzanne Kobasa and Salvatore Maddi [1] has shown that mental hardiness is a key factor in people who live high-stress lives but have a low illness rate. They handle stress better, both emotionally and physically This trait is not class-bound. The very poor who are emotionally hardy are as well stress-insulated as the rich who possess the same trait.

Mental hardiness is more an attitude toward life than a set of behaviors. Distill all the findings and four characteristics emerge as the core of mental hardiness. These are also central to the latest research on "EQ", emotional intelligence.

- Openesss to **Challenge** and **Change**
- Feeling of **Contribution** to and involvement in whatever one is doing.
- Sense of **Control** over life events
- **Commitment** to stable and continuing social networks

These factors characterize the Healthy Competitor, and are strengthened by the 8 Keys. But the competitor with a win-lose mindset is more mentally soft, regardless of how tough an opponent he may be. That's because the traits of mental hardiness are the most difficult for him to achieve. Let's see why:

- Change is often viewed as a threat to his position
- He often participates to gain power, position, posessions or prestige, having little interest in the activity itself.
- He too often lets others' moves determine his own actions
- He is suspicious, on guard for potential competition.

Mental softness, then, is embedded in lack of trust

in self and others and feelings of anxiety and insecurity. These are the win-lose competitor's frequent companions, especially if his competitive attitude spills over into his daily life.

When excellence is achieved and recognized, your status will come naturally. You will be recognized for your strength of character and/or the quality of your work. These factors have an intrinsic value about them, and are based on a rock-hard foundation upon which one can continually build. One-upmanship forms of status are, by definition, extrinsic. They depend not only on you, but also on how far your competitors climb on the ladder relative to you. Hence these forms of status are always up for grabs, which creates anxiety. Sooner or later, someone else will come along who can beat you and knock you out of the top slot. **The 8 Keys Competitor builds a castle, while the traditional competitor plays King of the Hill!**

Striving for significance, then, gives you the winning edge.

FINAL THOUGHTS

Today, "healthy competition" is about win-win, not win-lose.

"If you want to win, outserve your competition."
Arnold "Nick" Carter

OUTCOMES OF THE TWO MODELS
OF COMPETITION

KEY 1 - BASIC GOAL

**Traditional
Win-Lose Model**

"8 Keys" Model

BASIC GOAL:

STRIVE FOR SUPERIORITY

STRIVE FOR SIGNIFICANCE

* Be <u>the</u> best

   *   Be <u>your</u> best

Fear - sooner or later someone
better will beat you.

Confidence - you are unique
with a special mix of insights
and talents

ULTIMATE OBJECTIVE:

* Winning - beating opponents

   *   Contributing - making a
difference

WHAT YOU DO:

* Is secondary, or doesn't matter
as long as you win.
Ends justify means

   *   Is primary or critically important
Your actions are the vehicle for
your contribution.
Winning takes care of itself.

ENERGY USE:

* Disbursive - scattered
Easy to get off task,
Hooked on having to beat others,
cheating, or into negative ego issues.

   *   Intensive - focused
Stays on track
Motivated by sense of purpose

THE HEALTHY COMPETITION PARADOX
Strive for significance -
    * Do your very best
    * Make your greatest contribution
    * Use all of the resources at your command-
    and the winning will take care of itself.

INTRODUCTION TO KEY 1 - FOUNDATION

In today's society, competition has become a metaphor for living in general. As you learn how to compete, you automatically apply those lessons to life. The purpose and meaning in competition finds its basis in how you define "winning". Chances are, given our cultural conditioning, how you construe success in competing is pretty similar to how you see success in life as well.

To shift from attaining superiority to attaining significance as your definition of winning, as your underlying goal, is a quantum leap. For many folks, it amounts to nothing less than a conversion experience: an awakening that can change the course of your destiny. It involves a whole new, broader way of looking at life, the world, others, and ultimately yourself. It challenges you to see, think, and act in new ways and serves as a grounding for your other choices and actions. It boosts self esteem and emotional resilience. It's the first key emphasized in this book because it is fundamental. It's the common thread through all of the subsequent keys. When you have processed through all eight, you will come back to this one.

Why?

Because you will never have left it. Significance is at once the beginning, the end, and the journey.

Which way are you going? That depends on your desired final destination. This is where the road divides. Let's look at Significance in more detail.

 Key 1

**"You want to make your mark in this world?
Make a difference."**

H.A. Olson

**"That is happiness: to be dissolved into something
complete and great."**

Will Cather

**"True nobility is not found in one's blood nor bloodline
But in one's heart and in one's deeds."**

H.A. Olson

**"The difference between ordinary and extraordinary
is that little extra."**

Jon Goldman

**"If I lived just for myself,
without creating opportunities and salvation for people,
then I've lost the whole point of what life is about."**

Reggie White
Green Bay Packers

Chapter Five

KEY 1
BASIC GOAL (Purpose)

"BE SIGNIFICANT - MAKE A DIFFERENCE"

Excellence is critical - you won't have Significance without it. Yet excellence is just part of the story. The real source of the power of Significance lies elsewhere.

YOUR POWER COMES FROM YOUR PURPOSE

The people in this world who are most successful and happy are moved by a sense of purpose in life - a sense that life has meaning and they have an important role to play, a mission or destiny to fulfill. This sense of purpose, of meaning, is the common denominator, even though people's definitions of their own purpose may vary widely. Conversely, the people who are chronically unhappy, anxious or depressed almost invariably lack purpose. They are out of touch with their sense of direction in life.

Purpose is closely tied to your self-image, to your personal pride and courage. It strongly influences what you do with your bar, whether you play high jump or limbo.

Purpose is also the greatest stress-buster the world has ever seen. It provides staying power to help keep you going during the rough times. It brings meaning, joy - even excitement - to activities that might otherwise seem mundane.

Another subtle, but powerful, reason why most successful and happy people have a sense of purpose is that having a sense of purpose motivates success. Being fueled by a purpose about which you care helps to trigger your peak performance state. It makes the task seem easier, enhances focus and liberates your creativity. (See Keys 4-7.)

Faced with today's uncertainties, more than ever people want - and need - meaning in their lives. Purpose gives definition to your life, helping to make sense of the deeds you have done. Striving for significance fulfills purpose and makes it real.

Virtually everyone wants to make some mark in this world. People want to be important in some way, to leave some legacy behind so that they are remembered. No one wants to die anonymously, buried along with their name.

Significance goes far beyond competitive strategy. Fueled and guided by your sense of purpose, **being significant is how you make your mark**.

BUILD...

During the Middle Ages, a traveller once came to a particular city. He noticed many stone cutters busily at work. He went up to several and asked, "What are you doing?"

The first said, "I'm cutting stone. It's boring, but what the heck, another day, another dollar."

The second replied, "I'm the best stone-cutter in the country. Look how smooth this stone is, how perfect the edges are."

The third pointed to a foundation many yards away. "I'm building a cathdral."

How do you define what you do every day? What sense of purpose do you attach to your actions?

Guy Kawasaki, who's turning Apple Computer around, said, "People are motivated most when they have a sense they are making history, not just profits." [1]

SIGNIFICANCE - A DEFINITION

The total infusion of purpose and honor into mind, body and spirit, energizing and channeling ideas, feelings and actions, talents, assets and skills toward meeting needs in the service of a higher good.

In short: Making a Difference

Read over the definition of Significance a couple of times. Which words stand out as most important to you?

How do you make this definition **real**? How do you make it work in your life?

SIGNIFICANCE AT TWO LEVELS - LEVEL ONE

The first level is to do significant things. Significant acts or projects do not have to turn the whole world upside down. They can be very small in scope, and as simple as putting your arm around a grieving friend or helping in time of need. The key is that they make a useful contribution, create value and are **freely** given without a direct expectation of reward.

Ben and Jerry's, the Vermont-based ice cream manufacturer, has given literally tons of free ice cream to local fairs, festivals, and charitable fundraising activities. Giant Foods, a mid-Atlantic supermarket chain, donates computers and other equipment to schools upon receipt of a certain number of their cash register tapes. Many firms are turning green. They're donating, or shaping their policies and procedures to be sensitive to environmental concerns. Many individual business people volunteer countless hours to schools and community service organizations.

Lest we think that significance just means doing volunteer social service, consider Southwest Airlines. They have developed a thank-heaven-it's-Monday corporate culture. Part of the reason they are a rising star is that management and employees together have created a very positive, supportive, exciting and fun work environment for their own staff that encourages high levels of excellence in performance and production.

Sarah loves her job. She's a check-out parking fee collector on an airport overflow parking lot. While she admits the job is very routine, she gets great pleasure giving a smile, safe wishes, and occasional compliments to weary travelers as they drive through. They light up a bit in response. Sarah knows she's been of help.

"Lagniappe" (pronounced "Lan-yáhp") is a word commonly heard in New Orleans. It means "something extra", referring to some article or service given above and beyond the price paid. Lagniappe as a principle can be summed up as "Give more than you get" or "Go the extra mile", or "Whatever it takes". It imples both a high level of excellence and a solid concern for the people with whom you interact.

Let Lagniappe be the guiding principle for your daily activities and you will be pleasantly surprised at your increasing level of impact. This is not to say that you should let yourself be taken advantage of, however. There are predatory people out there who will use you if you let them. Significance has nothing to do with being a patsy nor a pushover, nor a workaholic. Protecting yourself and managing these situations will be handled in subsequent chapters.

The formula for Healthy Competition

$$W = E^3 + C_1 + C_2 + P$$

Winning equals Excellence plus Contribution plus Commitment plus Positioning. Excellence is elevated to the third power because it is the most critical aspect of the formula. Positioning refers to the activities required to create an effective image and to gain appropriate recognition. While we might like to think that this is unnecessary, positioning is usually critical for your contributions at work because of "office politics".

Contribution implies that there is a definite positive benefit and impact for others and the organization as a whole. Being totally excellent at something no one else needs or cares about will not mean as much on the job or in the other venues in which you are called upon to perform, regardless of how personally beneficial such excellence may be. Finally, commitment is the fire that keeps you going in the face of obstacles. Commitment is the emotional energy that gives you persistence and staying power. Commitment is fueled by your sense of purpose.

Mix these four qualities together and you have the essence of significance. As psychologist Edith Eger says, "What we do just for ourselves dies with us. What we do for others lives on." [2]

LEVEL TWO - WHAT KIND OF PERSON DO YOU WANT TO BE?

Ultimately, significance is more than what you do, it's what you are. Be significant rather than superior, be important rather than self-important. Significance is not a question of fame nor status, earning power nor the number or price of your possessions. Neither is significance simply a corporate or personal strategy. Nor is it tied to reward.

Rather, **significance is a personal quality**. A significant person exudes power, depth, sensitivity, and high character. Significance is not the same thing as charisma, however. Significant people have an abiding respect for others, their dignity, and their needs, whether or not they come across as charismatic. They are too big for petty politics and generous rather than jealous. They are virtuous. **Significance shows itself not only in what one does, but also in** how **one carries out daily tasks and responsibilities**.

Significance is generic. It can serve as the foundation for any positive purpose or goal. It can be exercised everywhere, every day. *It is the spirit you bring to your daily activities.*

Think of the significant people in history and in our current time. Gandhi, Eleanor Roosevelt, Abe Lincoln, Mary Kay Ashe, Churchill, Martin Luther King, Mother Theresa and Princess Diana, to name a few. How about the significant people you personally know. What traits do they have in common?

Stop reading for a moment. Reflect upon the people who have positively influenced **your** life in a special way. What did they do? How? Why do you remember those specific persons now?

In striving for significance, the healthy competitor doesn't compete by struggling to overcome an opponent, but by making his or her position positively **unassailable** - so solid, so vital, so excellent, that it is impossible to be overlooked. This actually requires so much less stress. As Coco Chanel said, "How many cares one loses when one decides not to be something but to be someone."[3]

The organization which strives for significance views "competitiveness" as being seen as **the most logical choice** by those both outside and **inside** the firm. Such an organization transcends the notion of "business is war" and begins to act on the unspoken premise that "business is love" toward both its customers and its own employees.

THE THREE PILLARS

Significance is founded upon three essential pillars: (A) **contribution** (B) a sense of **purpose, mission, and meaning in life**, and (C) **a high code of honor**. As stated earlier, most significant people feel a sense that they have been put here for a reason. They strive to make the most of what they have been given or to fulfill a destiny. (See Box

49

5.1 at the end of this chapter.) The relationship between significance, purpose and honor tends to be reciprocal. Purpose and honor enhance the striving for significance, which in turn increases one's sense of honor and purpose. As you make greater contributions and act honorably, you yourself become greater and more motivated. As we said earlier, your power lies in your purpose. **Significance, then, is the key to true importance and practical heroism**.

Johann Olav Koss was Norway's hero in the '94 Winter Olympics. Even so, he received more than his share of media coverage during and after the games. Why? He is a national hero in Norway, not only for his athletic prowess, but because of his humanitarian efforts. He donated monies resulting from his sports performance to Olympic Aid, and went on a mission to Eritrea to give sports equipment to schools there in hopes of attracting their school children into sports. Now he serves as a representative of UNICEF. **Whatever is worth doing, is worth doing significantly**.

LONG-HAUL WINNING

Striving for significance prepares you to continue to win over the long haul. It helps you to see the big, broad-range and long-term picture, and to see beyond immediate contests and demands to perform. It gives you staying power. Your efforts today become a future-oriented investment, not only in your organization or family, but in your own growth as well. Win or lose, your results in today's contest are solid preparation and practice for the next time around. As long as your definition of "winning" is not tied solely to the score, you can feel like a winner every time you must compete or perform!

THE GALLERY

Never underestimate the impact of the gallery, those who watch you from the sidelines. They can often make you or break you. Everything you do has an impact. As you become more significant, while some may become envious, generally you become more favored. More of the fans are pulling harder for you, cheering you on. Remember Nancy Kerrigan? Spectators from all over the world felt for her and wildly cheered her. That same audience only gave Tonya Harding polite applause and some even booed her in spite of the fact that Harding was a world class skater in her own right.

How do you think the fans' actions affect athletes before and during the competition? Often profoundly. Even when the score is the bottom line, being known as a significant person as well as a top athlete brings that much more audience acceptance and adoration even from fans of your opposition. Sensing this added support, knowing that the gallery is pulling for you, can significantly boost your confidence and give your performance that extra edge when the chips are down. Charles Austin, who won the 1996 Olympic Gold in high jump, claims the cheering crowd was

80% responsible for his victory. [4]   It also worked for Bonnie Blair and Dan Jansen, our 1994 Olympic speed skaters, and it can work for you. What goes around **does** come around.

Let's bring this idea home. How do you think a public speaker, an executive, a salesperson is affected by the behavior of the audience? Or by her *anticipation* of the behavior of the audience? As a public speaker, I know that I draw a great deal of energy from the audience. Subconsciously I and they have "collaborated" to make my presentation a success.

How do you think **you** are being affected by the attitudes of your coworkers? How do events at home affect work, and vice versa?

THE KEY TO YOUR INFLUENCE

Your credibility - your trusted name - is the ultimate key to your power and influence with others. Trust is the glue that holds organizations together and liberates people to do their best. If you lose credibility, you will lose influence and the favor and support of the gallery, no matter what position you hold or how much formal power you wield. Breaching trust is the hardest sin to forgive and forget.

As you strive for significance you will boost your credibility and admiration from those around you. You make your position that much more solid and unassailable. You also boost your leadership potential because people naturally will more readily follow a person in whom they can trust and believe. After all, people respond much more readily to what they perceive you to be rather than to what you do.

Michaelangelo carved exquisite statues, one chisel-tap at a time. Likewise you **build your reputation and make your mark one act at at time.**

DEEPER THAN ETHICS

Discussions on ethics in business and elsewhere are sorely needed. But to focus just on ethics is missing the mark. The real issue is **models**. What is your **model** - your basic paradigm or outlook - for competing, succeeding, managing your career, doing business, or living your life? **Your model drives your ethics.** If your model is "business is war" or to win at all costs, you will have quite a different ethical code in some areas than if your model is to strive for significance, the new model for healthy competition and success. As we said earlier, how you define winning is where the road divides. Each path has its own separate steps and logical conclusions. You will end up in a distinctly different place, depending on the path you choose.

Here's the bottom line. When you shift from striving for superiority to striving for significance you liberate yourself. You open yourself to many new opportunities and personal possibilities. Truly, the highest form of self-interest is interest in others. Meeting their needs is the best way to meet your own. **Performance becomes truly "peak" only when it has transcended duty and strategy, and has become a labor of love.**

BOX 5.1

THE QUALITIES OF THE MISSION-ARY

"Mission" - a passion and commitment to a cause larger than yourself.

When I was in college, I interviewed many missionaries and read the biographies of several more. As I looked at their lives and listened to their experiences, I noted six characteristics that the most successful missionaries had in common, that gave them the direction, drive, and staying power to thrive in the face of severe adversity.

- *Vision of human need and possibilities.* They have the ability to see something where now there is nothing. The mission is sparked with creativity and strong empathy.
- *Identification with a worthy cause.* They identify with something larger than themselves, which provides personal meaning.
- *Sense of one's own importance in promoting the cause.* This is not egotism but a healthy respect for one's role, talents, and capabilities. The greatness of the cause promotes a healthy humility.
- *Indestructible courage and commitment.* Do or die. These people possess the ability to hang in there no matter what.
- *Onward-outward orientation and drive.* They look for new avenues and opportunities of service. They have an expansionist orientation quite akin to that of many entrepreneurs.
- *Never-ending hope and faith.* This is the quality that provides the spark for mighty deeds.

You may have noticed that the first letters of these six-qualities spell VISION. No accident. All great endeavors begin with vision. Without it we are doomed to live in the darkness of our own shadows. Put all these qualities together, however, and miracles happen!

BOX 5.2

Play with this model for awhile.

"BUSINESS IS LOVE"

How do you treat a lover? Think back to a very special occasion with someone you really loved. Maybe it was a first date, or your wedding day, or a special time with your parents, children or a dear friend.

- What made that time so special?
- How did you treat that person?
- How did you feel about him or her at the moment?
- How did that person treat you?
- Why do you remember that event to this day?

    I'd bet that you:

- Were extremely attentive to that person's wishes and needs.
- Listened carefully to what he or she said.
- Went out of your way to do something special for him or her.
- Gave freely of yourself, your time, and your resources and didn't count the costs.
- Were creative in thinking up ways to make that person happy.
- Were attentive to the little details that would enhance your partner's pleasure.

What would happen if you treated your customers, employees, superiors, co-workers and suppliers and other shareholders in your company, and even your competitors, the very same way - without expecting them to treat you this way first?

Chapter Six

IMPLEMENTING KEY 1 EXERCISES

How you strive for significance is a very personal matter. No one can tell you what to do with your life. All lasting change and growth come from within. You are the expert on yourself. You have within yourself the answers you need.

"Purpose" and "Significance" can be understood and implemented at several levels, such as:

- General meaning and direction in life. This often has a spiritual or "higher calling" connotation.
- Specific direction of your energy toward particular goals or causes larger than yourself: eg. supporting your firm's vision and mission, creating or supporting a business or social cause, solving a personal problem or issue of your own and then helping others with similar concerns. (This is what Alcoholics Anonymous and similar groups have done.)
- Improving the quality of life where you work and live through your personal attitude and actions.
- Doing the best job you can in whatever you do.
- Being a solid, dependable, contributing team or family member.

The exercises for this and the other seven keys can help guide your thinking and action, and help you release and fulfill your potential.

(1).   **Write out your sense of purpose or mission**, perhaps in the form of a personal mision statement. **Redefine** your career, professional or personal goals in terms of making a difference.

(2).   **Clarify your core values**. Try specifying them and writing them out. What are your key beliefs and attitudes that guide your behavior?

(3).   **Create your personal honor code**. Spell out a few statements starting with "on my honor, I will..." that serve as a daily guide for thought and action. Read them every morning and carry them with you.

(4).   **Review your strengths list**. Which of these can become a vehicle, guide, or channel: an outlet for increased contribution and value, for making improvements?

(5).   **Get involved**. Help out.

(6).   **Develop and put into practice a specific contribution plan** that is uniquely yours or your team's, that will add value, make improvements, and touch lives where you are right now. Make it personally challenging. Excitment lies at the cutting edge.

(7).   **Be significant**. Could it be that these two words sum up the ultimate purpose of enterprise and meaning of life? Define yourself as a totally "significant person". Spell out what that means in your own terms. Build this concept into your self-image.

AFFIRMATIONS FOR KEY 1

STOP! If you have not used affirmations or visualizations before, read Appendix I before continuing.

Here are some affirmations for Key 1. You can use some of these or make up your own.

I am significant
I am the soul of honor
My word is my bond
I can be counted on whenever necessary
I do unexpected deeds of kindness
My honor is love
I make a difference every day
I preserve the honor and dignity of others
I love life, life loves me
As I give, I shall receive
Excellence is my code in all that I do
I treat all others as I wish to be treated
I am virtuous

VISUALIZATIONS FOR KEY 1

1. TARGETED STREAM OF CONSCIOUSNESS -
    Let your mind and imagery wander around the
    notion of yourself as fully significant. Let your
    creative subconscious have full, unfettered reign.
    What images and ideas come to mind? Do any
    patterns emerge? Do any new directions for your
    energies come forward?

2. MENTAL REHEARSAL - Visualize yourself
    carrying out your contribution plan. Imagine all the
    details. See everyone benefitting and imagine the
    appropriate recongnition you will receive. Let the
    positive feelings sink in.

3. MOTIVATOR - Imagine yourself inspiring,
    empowering, leading or helping others.

   Now that you have begun to think and act in terms
of increased contribution, it's critical to be able to release
all your powers. In order to accomplish this, you need to
begin with how you define yourself. This leads us on to
Key Two - the next step in our journey.

FINAL THOUGHTS

Don't get hung up on what is; rather focus on what you strive to be.

"Be the change you want to see happen in the world."

Gandhi

The things that really count in life are those that you take with you when you die, or leave behind in the hearts, minds, and spirits of others.

What kind of person do you want staring back at you in the mirror each day?

61

The 8 Keys to Becoming Wildly Successful and Happy

Introduction to Keys 2, 3, & 4
Courage/Emotional Self-Reliance

The resilience and interdependence required for career and personal success go much deeper than strategy. They are personal qualities. **Courage** is the rock upon which these qualities are founded.

Courage, however, is not always doing flashing deeds of derring-do, taking wild risks, or having no fear. Let's be honest. Fear and uncertainty often accompany any change and growth. We all get afraid at times.

True courage is the ability to:

- "Just Do It" - Meet life's challenges head-on, take appropriate risks, break through what's holding you back

- Stand up and speak out for what is right, even in the face of tough opposition

- Take full personal responsibility for one's thoughts, feelings and actions

- Proactively follow through

- Manage and limit fear so that positive purpose drives thought, feeling and action

- Be flexible and be able to openly admit when we're wrong

- Be authentic: be yourself and be open to people

- In short - make the most of what you have - your talents, strengths, resources, skills and limitations.

This definition isn't glamorous, but it's where the rubber meets the road. It takes a big person to demonstrate this kind of courage. How big do you want to be?

Courage is actually a habit of mind. It requires and is built upon emotional self-reliance. This is the second "S-word" that characterizes true champions. The first is Significance. Strive for Significance in all you do, be a Significant person. This enhances your ease at accomplishing the next three keys, and the next three help you to fulfill the first one. Purpose creates Passion, which fuels Courage.

Keys 2, 3, and 4 are the courage-building keys. They are closely linked, focusing on achieving high levels of emotional self-reliance. Key 2 deals with liberation from internal self-defeating fear, shame and ego traps. Key 3 deals with rising above comparison, external standards of worth and pressures to conform, and self-limiting habits and thoughts. Key 4 is the transition key. It deals with developing a more optimistic, expansive attitude that promotes greater creativity and more positive energy. Since energy is determined by perception, Key 4 is the natural bridge to the Energy/Action Keys 5, 6 and 7.

Mastering Keys 2, 3 and 4 is critical for productive teamwork and leadership, especially in self-directed work teams and virtual organizations. While they rarely describe their culture in these terms, truly cutting edge organizations encourage courageous behavior throughout the firm. In organizations where re-engineering and other improvement efforts fail, the unspoken root causes quite often reflect difficulties in the realm of these three keys.

The strongest teams are always composed of "strong" individuals in the sense of solid self-esteem, emotional security, and inner tranquility - high Key 2, 3 and 4 outcomes. Teamwork works best when individuals have risen above fear, envy, and ego limitations and are therefore ready, willing and able to give their best for the common good.

Much is being written on the importance of "emotional intelligence" (EQ) as critical to one's success. While the whole 8 Keys Model teaches EQ, Keys 2-4 provide the emotional/ behavioral foundation for its development.

The 8 Keys to Becoming Wildly Successful and Happy

Key 2

**The first step in being open to life
is to get past yourself."**

H.A. Olson

**"The one important thing I have learned over the years
is the difference between taking one's work seriously
and taking one's self seriously.
The first is imperative, and the second is disastrous."**

Margot Fonteyn
Prima
Ballerina

"Develop the courage to be imperfect."

Rudolf Dreikurs

Chapter Seven

KEY 2
SELF-DEFINITION
"Be yourself - be ego-flexible."

Why are we so often reluctant to change, or to be all that we can be? Why do we sometimes shoot ourselves in the foot just as we come near the finish line? Why do our best efforts sometimes go awry, when according to logic and circumstances they should succeed? Why do we procrastinate or hold ourselves back?

We have all heard great ideas or methods that initially inspired us. Maybe we experienced a fantastic training program, and we couldn't wait to use the new information. But on Monday morning, when we got back to "reality", we never implemented them.

The self-concept resists change. Those new ideas got rationalized away or forgotten - absorbed into an existing self/ego system that rendered them ineffective. Why?

There are many reasons why good information doesn't "stick": Lack of organizational support for new learning, ineffective training methods, the "comfort zone", etc. Much of the problem at a personal level, however, involves the conflict between Will and Imagination. We Will to grow, but if we find ourselves holding back, deep inside we most likely Imagine that our self-perceived inadequacies will be exposed.

THE 4 GREAT FEARS

Look. Fear accompanies almost any new challenge. We all experience it.

The greatest social fears that plague peak performers are **humiliation**: if we try, we may be ridiculed, criticized or laughed at. **Rejection:** if we try, others may not like or approve of us, put us down, or say "no". **Failure**: if I try, I may lose, fail, look weak or incompetent. **Success**: if I try, I may actually succeed!

"Fear of Success" is subtle and sinister because society says we're supposed to **want** success, not fear it. Therefore, it's probably the most secret fear of all. If other people don't talk about fear, and I'm afraid, then I may think "Am I the only odd ball? What's wrong with me?"

Fear of success is actually very pervasive. Studies show that as many as 70% of high achievers fear success to some degree, for a variety of reasons. Some feel that down deep they don't deserve success, that they are really phony. Some think that their rise was "luck" or a "fluke" - that they won't be able to sustain their success. Some fear that their

69

weaknesses will be exposed, or that their friends will turn on them or envy them. Others fear facing fiercer competition. They figure it's better to be the biggest fish in the pond than to swim in the ocean . . . with sharks. The common cause is self-doubt.

Success-fearers show certain tendencies. They often start off gung-ho, then slack off or make more mistakes when they get closer to the goal. They may not be happy or excited when they succeed. They may minimize their successes and talents.

THE ULTIMATE FEAR

If any of these feared circumstances comes to pass, it may result in our feeling **shamed**. Shame is the one emotion that can lead us to feel an overall sense of reduced competence. When you lose confidence in one area you often begin to lose it in other areas also.

The drive to avoid shame is innate. It is biologically programmed, and is almost as strong as our need for air and water. It is usually stronger than our desire to succeed. If we fear shame enough, we will avoid risking it even at the cost of our success. (See Appendix 4)

The 4 Fears and Shame are particularly problematic because they most occur **when we are expressing ourselves or experimenting**. Thus we avoid by holding back, making excuses, procrastinating, not following through, rationalizing, etc. Shame shuts down creativity.

Rarely do we recognize that **the true cause for our self-limitation lies in our fear to release our full power**.

The fear of shame is the world's main killer of peak performance. Everyone who would succeed in life must learn to nullify its power.

The antidote to shame is not to deny it, fight onward or tough it out, but to **reduce our definition of what is shameful**. This is accomplished in two ways: (A) increasing our positive pride and faith in our skills and in ourselves, and (B) minimizing the emotional threat-potential of the feared outcome.

Suppose I fear bombing a public speech. I can get coaching and improve my skills, I can also redefine the emotional impact of bombing from "perceived catastrophe" to "undesirable, but no big deal."

THE ROOT OF COURAGE

It takes **courage** to become all that you can be, and to be your authentic self. . . Courage requires self-confidence. . . Self-confidence is built upon **self-acceptance. Accepting yourself as you are right now is the first step to growth and to high self-esteem.**

THE ANTIDOTE TO SELF-LIMITATION

Shame and social fear are **ego-issues**. It's the ego that becomes afraid. Nothing else. For example, if I feel

71

insulted or rejected, it's my ego that's hurt, not me. Therefore, reducing fear and releasing our full potential depends on being able to **get our egos out of the way** when the chips are down. Our egos can become our greatest barrier.

The value of the ego is inversely proportional to the importance of the task.

Most of us have egos like crystal punch bowls - big and fragile. I know I do, and over the years it has cost me big-time. "Ego" is human nature. None of us can become fully ego-free, but if we want to maximize our success, we need to manage our egos to best advantage. Why?

Part of the ego's task is self-protection. Its job is to compensate for shame and the inner feelings of inferiority and self-doubt that plague all of us to some degree. With the changing economy, downsizing, and increased demands for put-up-or-shut-up excellence, most of us are more insecure and scared than ever. We especially fear slipping up and looking foolish or inept. The potential for shame is greater.

When insecurity, shame, or criticisms may make us feel little, it's the ego's job to make us feel big, important. It strives to preserve and protect our image to the world, and to hide our inadequacies from public view, and from ourselves as well. The ego keeps our guard up and walls certain other people out.

THE EGO CAN CONFUSE OUR PRIORITIES

When the ego gets out of hand, it can lead to arrogance and vanity. It creates a felt need to be superior to others. It denies the reality of our inner fear experience. How can I fix something if I deny its existence?

Ego also promotes suspiciousness, envy, jealousy, dishonesty, hostility and rivalry. The ego leads us to become more shallow as persons, while our true answers lie in our depth.

To the ego, the best defense is often an offense. The ego often overpersonalizes situations and leads us to take things too seriously. "Feedback" is too often seen as "criticism". If left totally to its own devices, the ego can only be satisfied when it makes us the center of the universe. So much for "teamwork" when the ego's in the driver's seat!

The problem which the ego creates for peak performance is that ego-based superiority is external image-oriented and requires the approval and admiration of others. This creates added fragility, tension and pressure to "win" or to look good - and **increases the potential for shame** if we don't! Thus the ego distracts us from the main task, which is to perform at our best.

It also leads us to listen selectively. The ego hears only what it wants to hear, and risks rejecting needed information. When the ego holds sway, it can severely interfere with our ability to heed advice or to self-correct when we're going down a wrong track. Sometimes it leads us to kill the messenger. Our egos can make us rigid and resistant to change. Ego also lies behind excessive perfectionism. Worse, our egos can make us **unteachable**.

The ego can also cause us to be unforgiving and to impair key relationships in the process of being "right" or having the last word. In short - when our egos are hooked, we are more easily threatened - and thus more likely to attack, destroy or flee from what, or who, threatens us.

THE "TRIPLE ERROR"

Our culture has snookered us again. Down through history it has preached the "triple error" as gospel truth:

1. We are not good nor worthy enough as we are
2. Our worth as persons is determined by our performance
3. Our worth is relative to where we stand compared to others.

The 4 Fears and Shame have their root in the Triple Error.

The ego creates a fragile self image because it buys into the Triple Error completely. Then it erects an image-front to counter it. The ego supports the notion that our worth is conditional and that we must prove ourselves to others. Thus **the ego promotes fear!**

Granted, in a job it's realistic to have to prove certain capabilities, and perhaps to compete, but let's never confuse that with the idea of proving our worth as persons, or tying our intrinsic worth to the outcomes of any one contest or task. **As long as one feels he must "prove himself", he is never truly free.**

Achieving ego-flexibility and true courage, then, depends in part in our ability to let go of the Triple Error: to recognize our worth as intact and unassailable, independent of any specific performance. That's the way to positive pride.

EGO-FLEXIBILITY

The mindset of ego-flexible persons is truly liberating. Self esteem, self worth and self acceptance are high. Ego-flexible folks separate their worth from their performance and know that they are worthwhile just as they are. They have solid faith in themselves and their talents. They can also be more open to spirituality in their lives if they so choose. Because they are not as hung up on external issues such as image and status, they can be more "real" and "open", often demonstrating greater "depth" to their lives.

Therefore, ego-flexible people have less to fear or protect. They are more invulnerable. They can be non-defensive and can remain undaunted in the face of rejection, criticism, put-downs or negative circumstances. They bounce back quicker.

Ego-flexible people radiate honesty, sincerity and genuine warmth. They are often more interesting and enjoyable to be around. They make better friends.

EGO-FLEXIBLE WORK

When faced with a challenge, their first thought is "What must I do to accomplish the task or solve the problem?" Because they accept their worth as independent of performance, they are less worried about success and failure. They are free to welcome change and to experiment with new ideas and methods.

Ego-flexible people are more focused. They stick to their knitting and remain ever conscious of their purpose. Work becomes an opportunity to shine, to try out new strategies, to succeed. They take mistakes in stride, viewing them as vital learning opportunities. They learn all they can.

They are also free to cooperate, share, and contribute to the total team effort. They are more willing to help others, and share credit and leadership. Ego-flexible people recognize that if their team wins, they win also. While ego-invested people often see others as a threat, ego-flexible people see others as their greatest resource.

A FRESH PERSPECTIVE

While performance may vary, our worth is intrinsic. We are all of equal worth. We are all worth 1. No one is worth 1½, nor ¾. The mystery of creation is that we are all given different capabilities in differing proportions. Therefore, we each have some pieces of the total puzzle. Our task is to find others with different pieces and to work together to put those pieces in place. As long as we fear differences in others, doubt our own worth or must always control, we can never accomplish the task.

No one piece is more important, because **all pieces are required**. And . . . working cooperatively drives out fear.

WHO'S THE BOSS?

The job, that's who. The ultimate determiner of success is **meeting or exceeding the requirements of the task**. Relative worth of capability or skill only makes sense in terms of what skills or talents are required to do the job. If the job changes, new or different skills may be required. That's all.

Are any one set of skills or talents "better" than another? For the needs of a particular task, yes. I'm a psychologist. For doing personal coaching, my skills are beneficial. But if I were to tackle an engineering problem, I'd fail miserably. I have little skill in that area. Does any of this make me a better or worse **person**? Or more or less **worthy**? **Never!** The playing field of personal worth is always level.

The 8 Keys to Becoming Wildly Successful and Happy

Chapter Eight

IMPLEMENTING KEY 2 EXERCISES

A beloved mentor of mine, Harold Mosak, once said of ego, self-esteem and fear, "**It's all fiction**. Which fiction do you wish to believe?"

Developing greater courage and positive pride, then, is a matter of changing self-limiting fictions - ideas and perceptions that hold us back. That happens best when we **combine new ways of looking with new ways of acting.**

(1)   **Learn to recognize when your ego is getting in your way.** The descriptions in the last and the next chapter will help, as will Box 8.1 at the end of this chapter. Then **keep your ego out of your major decisions and actions** as best you can.

(2)   **Develop a clearer understanding of your own goodness.** Not just what you're "good at", but your innate goodness as a person. You might start by reviewing your assets list from Chapter 3 and adding to it now. Think about how your goodness and talents show up in everyday behavior, and notice and appreciate them when they occur. Give yourself permission to value yourself just as you are today. This is **positive pride**.

79

(3)   **Stay mission-focused rather than me-focused**. Put your energy into contribution. Draw your gratification and importance from that and the rest will follow. True importance comes from actions, not self-praise.

(4)   **Learn all you can**, both in your field and in other areas related to it. Many folks are overwhelmed by "information overload" and avoid training. They fear that new knowledge will show up what they don't know, exposing felt inadequacies. Don't scare yourself with what you don't know. Be confident you will learn what you need to know. Make learning a quest. Set up a personal learning contract with goals. Get started.

(5)   **Develop true humility**. Humility isn't denying your strengths, putting yourself down, or being embarrassed by compliments. Rather, it's an attitude of gratitude. It's a feeling of thankfulness for the power and opportunity to succeed, and for the recognition you might have received. Truly humble people don't contribute just for the recognition, but if recognition comes they can enjoy it. Thank people openly when they help you in any way.

(6)   **Learn to laugh at yourself**. No one enjoys jokes or barbs at their expense, but good clean fun is no threat. If we learn to see and accept our blunders and imperfections as natural and OK, our self-esteem will grow. One who can laugh at oneself is truly invulnerable. A bird soars because it can take itself lightly!

(7)　**Don't take things too personally**. Separate your worth from performance. You are not your job. Distinguish "refusal" from "rejection". Ignore the little digs of life. Let them roll off your back rather than dwelling on them. Develop a healthy perspective as to what's important in the long run and what isn't. Avoid one-upmanship, always having to have the last word, and feeling like you always have to prove yourself. **Just do your best - that's proof enough**.

(8)　**Increase your approachability**. Help others to be more comfortable around you. Listen carefully. Be appropriately lavish with compliments and your appreciation. Smile. Ask questions and accept feedback. Get help and advice. Don't be afraid to touch others physically in appropriate ways, such as a hand on a shoulder or pat on the back. Don't be afraid to hug. Volunteer your aid. Admit when you're wrong. Laugh and be playful. Wear a smile. Refuse to be a complainer or participate in gossip. (You don't want a reputation of being "down" or a "tale-carrier".) Be friendly and willing to listen to all, regardless of job, status, race or other distinctions. The list goes on. You get the idea. Pay attention to how you come across. Does your style best suite your purpose?

(9)　**Develop a "character sketch" of Courageous You**. Describe yourself as more courageous in your own terms. What would you be like? What would you do? How would you act? Write this out. Read it frequently. Actively visualize yourself behaving this way in tough situations.

(10) Strive for excellence, not perfection. Perfectionism can slow you down and keep you from getting started on new projects. It sets you on a quest for the impossible and leads only to frustration. Redefine "perfect" as "meeting or exceeding requirements".

(11) Face your fears realistically. Look at your job. Are there tasks or changes you're resisting or uncomfortable doing? Identify these and honestly name any fear that might be underlying your discomfort, eg. "making cold phone calls - fear of rejection". Get past your rationalizations. Then ask yourself what is objectively likely to happen. Debate your exaggerations, reminding yourself of your positive strengths and capabilities you bring to the situation.

(12) Start taking appropriate risks. At your own pace, begin to do what you fear. How else can you discover your true strength? Identify specifically what you're afraid of and develop a specific plan to overcome or get beyond it. If any of your acquaintances have similar concerns, try doing it together.

(13) Work on the rest of the 8 Keys. They also support ego-flexibility. Ego-flexibility doesn't happen overnight. Some areas of your life may be more flexible than others. You know best where you need to put your energy.

(14) Do what you're proud of, be proud of what you do.

82

AFFIRMATIONS FOR KEY 2

Affirmations and visualizations are extremely powerful tools for broadening one's self-concept and for developing courage. Make heavy use of these at this point.

I act courageously
I am myself in every situation
My worth is total, complete and certain.
I tune into and use my goodness, talents and strengths more
     every day.
I celebrate the beauty and strength within myself and
others.
I am a true friend.
My confidence soars.
I discover and act out my inner power every day.
I am totally calm, confident, and secure.
I overcome fear.
I am totally worthy of others' love and respect.
I am a person of significance, defined by love.
Ego melts away. I'm free to be totally myself.

VISUALIZATIONS FOR KEY 2

1.   Visualize a past success. See yourself at the point of your success. Re-feel those feelings of pride, power and satisfaction that you had initially. (Do this image alone, or follow it immediately with image 2 or 3 below.)

2.   Visualize yourself handling a tough or feared situation courageously and effectively. See yourself being confident, assertive, maintaining self-control. See the situation coming out the way you want it to. Use your Courageous You character sketch.

3.   Mentally rehearse yourself being yourself, opening up more in a work or social situation, letting go of ego-barriers. See others respecting, liking and appreciating you for your naturalness and humanity. See yourself and them feeling closer.

FINAL THOUGHTS

You can only succeed when you're not afraid to fail.

"There is no limit to what a person can do or where he can go, if he doesn't mind who gets the credit."

Emerson

In the sixth century BCE, Lao-Tzu said of the leader:
> "He is a catalyst, and although things wouldn't get done as well if he weren't there, when they succeeded, he takes no credit. And **because he takes no credit, credit never leaves him**." (1)

"O wad some spirit the giftie gie us,
To see oursels as ithers see us.
It wad from many a blunder free us,
And foolish notion."
Robert Burns

Love and positive pride cast out fear. Thus, these are the best antidotes to shame and the best producers of real courage.

Box 8.1

YOU CAN BET YOUR EGO'S INVOLVED
WHEN YOU . . .

Worry about who's getting ahead.

Put image ahead of substance.

Feel jealous, get even, fight.

Show off to impress others.

Let what others think interfere with otherwise
positive action.

Jockey for power.

Compare yourself with others (other than to learn
and grow).

Over-concern yourself with evaluation.

Feel you must keep up with the Joneses.

Feel competitive when there is no actual contest.

Feel you must **win** rather than simply achieve.

Feel superior to others, or put them down.

Take excessive risk, or put yourself in harm's way
unnecessarily.

Act judgmentally or morally superior to others.

Gossip, carry tales, or backbite.

Have to have the last word.

Persist in an argument that should be ended.

Fool yourself about any of the above.

86

 Key 3

"True independence is the ability to
(A) freely act upon informed choice and
(B) to share and accept help in any appropriate network
without feeling threatened."

H.A.Olson

"The only time you have any real chance of success
is when you play the game your own way."

Harvey Ruben

"Contrary to popular belief,
there are no victims in this world -
only willing participants.
You can't always control your circumstances,
but you can control how you respond to them.
And everyone has the power to change at any
time...They can take away everything else, but they can
never take the treasures in your mind."

Edith Eva Eger, Ph.D.
Psychologist, Auschwitz
survivor

"To thine own self be true."

Anon.

Chapter Nine

KEY 3
CENTER OF CONTROL

"CALL YOUR OWN SHOTS"

Who's beating the drum to which you march? Who's calling the shots for your actions and feelings? Are you an imitator or an initiator?

Having a solid sense of Internal Control (IC) is **basic** to your success and happiness. It's central to self-reliance and resilience, and to maintaining high-quality relationships.

Yet, today in our anxious society, our collective sense of IC has never been lower. Personal insecurity and feelings of external control are at an all-time high. Why do you think we're so interested in psychics and angels?

PERSONAL POWER

IC isn't about who's your boss at work or who writes your paycheck. Rather "Center of Control" is a **self-determination continuum**. It involves the degree to which you take personal charge over your own thoughts, feelings and actions Vs handing off your power or letting others pull your strings. It involves being personally resourceful Vs depending on others, things, or circumstances to make you happy, satisfied, or successful. It often involves "getting unstuck". Center of Control is rooted in **how we think**. It helps to shape our world-view, attitudes and values. It's directly tied to our self image and self esteem. Therefore it strongly influences how we cope and function every day. It even determines our perception of our options.

"GOOD FENCES MAKE GOOD NEIGHBORS"

When Robert Frost penned those words, he wasn't talking about real estate. IC Vs External Control (EC) is about positive **behavioral and emotional boundaries** between ourselves and the outside world. It's about setting healthy personal limits which in turn preserves your freedom.

Healthy "problem ownership" is also involved. This refers to recognizing which situations you have responsibility for and which you do not. You "own" any problem that has a **concrete, tangible effect** upon you. Handling it is your task. Regardless of how personally troubling it may be to you, if someone else's situation has no direct tangible effect on you, it "belongs" to them. You may choose to care, listen or give support, but it's their job to deal with it. Not yours.

Much of the stress and burnout we experience comes as a result of our failure to build, mend, or honor our fences.

HIGH IC

Folks high on IC feel that they are the masters of their fate, that their outcomes are in large measure the result of their own actions. They are self confident, secure and encouraged.

They can take full responsibility for their own actions and can control their feelings and impulses well. They can delay gratification when necessary. Because they feel in control of themselves and are emotionally independent, they have less need to have (or force) outside circumstances to go their way. They're better able to roll with life's punches and bounce back. They are more positively assertive. They also tend to be richer and better educated. They make their own luck.

High IC sometimes gets confused with having to be a "rock" (nothing bothers me), "superman" (I can do it all by myself) or above proper authority (the rebel). Those attitudes are actually External Control (EC) in reverse! Feigning strength while fearing getting help is a common practice. Yet it is often driven by Key 2 errors such as fears of getting emotionally close, losing face or exposing one's weaknesses. Rocks, rebels and supermen are brittle and defensive on power and control issues, whereas High IC people can be more flexible and cooperative.

Emotional detachment does not mean "I don't care". High IC folks can be genuinely caring and compassionate **because of good boundaries**. They empathize, yet don't let

90

themselves get consumed in others' troubles. They recognize that each person is responsible for his or her own outcomes.

High IC people are free to be mutually interdependent. They can share, expose their weaknesses to the right people at the right time if necessary. They can freely ask for and receive appropriate help. They can listen to others and change their minds if they think someone else has a better idea. They can be strong for others and at times let others be strong for them. In short, **they can be fully human**.

Total self-sufficiency is as much a myth as total dependency. We all need to rely on others at times, as well as to think and act for ourselves. We all want to be powerful in some way, yet we also want to be nurtured. High IC lets us have both.

HIGH EC

Externally controlled people are more **re**-active, more easily triggered into instantly responding to events without giving proper thought to their actions. Others can press their hot buttons with relative ease. Often they are more dependent and imitative, caving in to peer pressure or needing to keep up with the Joneses. They rely more on others, things, substances or outside circumstances to make them happy or secure. They often define success in society's or other's terms rather than in their own. **They**

feel less in charge of their actions and their lives. Their emotional boundaries are much more permeable.

As a result, they frequently feel more helpless, vulnerable, and more easily threatened. Despite outward self-assurance, down deep they have less self confidence. They see their power as conditional. They doubt their ability to handle tough challenges, to buck the tide, handle intimidating people, or overcome troubling issues from the past. Thus, they often must have outside circumstances go their way in order to feel secure. They may feel like victims or like puppets on a string.

SYMPTOMS OF EC

EC symptoms are all **reactions**. They are varied and far reaching. Many are actually "human nature" and we've all experienced most of them at times. High EC people do some of them more habitually or to greater degree. They more frequently feel like they "can't help it" or "The Devil made me do it." Taken to extremes, these symptoms can wreak havoc.

Symptoms include excuse-making and buck-passing, blaming others whenever anything goes wrong, imitation and Jones-chasing, envy, jealousy, hostility and explosive temper, violence, impulsiveness, overdependence and submissiveness, excessive competitiveness, struggle to control others or outside circumstances, and fears of commitment or cooperation or involvement with others.

Also included are addictions, anxiety and depressive or compulsive thoughts and impulses which we can't seem to shake off. "External" doesn't mean "outside oneself". It means "outside one's perceived control". Internal "forces" can plague us even more than outside events. In fact, most of today's mental health concerns involve EC issues.

EC and IC are relative. In some areas we may demonstrate greater IC, while in other areas we are more externally controlled.

The Touchstone for Truth when we're engaging in EC-related behavior is how free we think we are to feel or do otherwise. **Must** we do these things, or can we be equally comfortable with ourselves if we **don't** do them? Consider conforming (or drinking), for example. If I choose to act or dress like others because **I** really like or enjoy it, OK. But if I do it primarily to relieve internal or peer pressure, because **I** fear criticism, or to gain status or approval, (or if I'm kidding myself about this), I may be too externally controlled.

POWER-SAPPING TRAPS

The real traps don't occur outside. They exist between our ears. The traps that follow are commonplace, natural tendencies. Since they are supported by our culture, they're easy to fall into, and can quickly become habits of mind. Yet they will hinder your performance, undermine your feelings of self-worth, eat you out inside, and rob you of inner peace.

93

(1) **Invidious Comparisons** "Invidious" means hateful, provoking of anger or jealousy. Invidious comparison is one of our greatest causes of dis-ease, discouragement and insecurity. It's the root of envy and jealousy and much of our brooding, hostility and competitiveness. These attitudes teach us to focus our minds on others rather than on our own concerns and possibilities.

Most often, invidious comparison involves comparing our weaknesses with others' strengths, or what we think we lack with what someone else has. When we do this, we're usually not conscious of what we're really doing. We think we're just checking to see where we stand relative to others.

Actually we're **selectively** comparing. We focus on one area or point of comparison (e.g. looks, income, status or possessions), blow it up out of proportion, make it the main defining standard of our worth, and believe our conclusions to be actual fact. Then we eat ourselves up inside unless and until we surpass the person with whom we're comparing ourselves.

Invidious comparison promotes **deficit thinking**. When we focus on what we **lack**, we can never fully realize nor be happy with what we **have**. Little by little, then, our sense of worth and satisfaction is pulled outside of ourselves. Our "inner core" - our sense of self, self esteem, self image - becomes diminished. Worse, it becomes **relative** to where others stand. Certain others then become our standard bearers, and the ones to beat. This leads to imitation and keeping up with the Joneses.

This is how jealousy begins. If I'm jealous of someone, I'm actually giving that person a certain degree of power over my feelings of worth, taking that power away from myself. Jealousy makes us hostile. Jealousy, envy and hostility are three of the greatest emotional killers of peak performance and personal happiness. At the extreme, they are forms of insanity. They are really red herrings, occurring when our egos get hooked into comparing and in having to struggle to prove our superiority, or to win.

(2) **Hostility** The purpose of anger is to tell us something needs to be corrected. It usually occurs when we're feeling hurt or out of control. As long as we solve the root problem, our anger has been helpful. Too often, however, it leads to hostility and the desire to punish others.

Whatever we attack, we (A) **fear,** (B) **honor** with our time, attention and energy, (C) **give it credence** and validity, and (D) **perpetuate** by keeping the fight going and investing it with some of our own power. **Whenever we attack others, we actually attack ourselves first.** We're more hurt in the long run by our hostility than our opponents are. Who suffers the inner turmoil, stress, high blood pressure, embarassment or other consequences of our hostile acts? Besides, the best "revenge" is to rise above, not to let our opponents continue to hook our feelings and actions.

95

(3)   **Craving For Approval** (Fear of Rejection) This is the root of peer pressure, and can also lead to intimidation, imitation and conformity. We all want to be liked, but it's a mistake to feel we must be **always** approved, adored or admired by certain others - or by everyone - **in order to** feel worthwhile.

Approval-cravers learned early in life that they are not good enough unless they please others. (The Triple Error again!) They've carried that extra burden throughout life, even though the basic notion of constantly needing to please is irrational and self-destructive.

(4)   **Victim Mentality**   Many of us have been "victimized" in life: through downsizing, losing a job, financial reversals, being a victim of violence or emotional/physical/sexual abuse. Perhaps we've been ill or physically injured, leaving us physically impaired. Maybe we've been victims of prejudice or unfair treatment. Much can happen to us that is outside of our direct control, "unfair" and not our fault.

Yet, the greatest damage occurs if we begin to **see ourselves as victims**. This is how Voodoo works. "Victim" is a **mindset** that denies and limits our true power. We begin to feel unfairly trapped, that there's no way out. We may continue to let difficult people intimidate us. We also may begin to view our world **unidimensionally,** as if what we're victim of becomes the lens through which we view our whole life.

For example, being "downsized" is normally a shocking thing. But I truly undercut myself if I begin to feel inadequate, less worthy, less valuable, or more vulnerable as a result. Or I may not like some parts of my job. But I really limit myself if I feel there's nothing I can do to make it better.

A "victim" is anyone who believes that others or outside circumstances are responsible for one's current state. Thus victims usually wait for, and demand, that **others** change first. The victim mentality paralyses action.

THE COMMON FALLACY . . .

To these traps is the tendency to put others' heads higher than our own. Thus we magnify others' worth, value, threat, or impact while diminishing our own. Thus, we hand off our power to others, and remain hooked, under their power by our own choice.

To compensate by struggling to be superior to others, or to get even, will not solve the problem. Neither will continuing to prove ourselves or to have to please. Those just keeps us locked in. The answer lies in developing our own inner resources and emotional freedom. This indirectly brings others down to size. It permits us to view ourselves as equals, and others with appropriate respect.

TAKING BACK YOUR POWER

For better or worse, **what ever you think about long enough, often enough, ultimately controls you.** Think about the right things. Then you can take the right actions.

Taking back your power starts with the recognition that you **have** power, **considerable** power, regardless of how well you've used it up to now. **Assume your strength, then you will find your strength**.

The first step in regaining power is "changing your mind": relearning, viewing yourself in a new light, and increasing your self-determination. It means taking full responsibility for your own thoughts, feelings and actions, altering them as needed and letting go of that which is holding you back or which isn't your concern.

FINAL THOUGHTS

Externally controlled success seekers wrap themselves around success. Internally controlled success seekers wrap success around themselves.

You can't be let down if you haven't been leaning on."
Walter "Buzz" O'Connell

"Finally, beloved, whatever is true, , whatever is honorable, whatever is just, whatever is pure, whatever is pleasing, whatever is commendable, if there is any excellence and if there is anything worthy of praise, think about these things."
St. Paul

BOX 9.1
AN EXAMPLE - AND A QUIZ

Think through the following poem, "The Whole Truth" by Judith Viorst

He always called her honey and
She always called him sweetie and
He always brought her flowers and
She always stroked his hair.
Their beautiful relationship was
What a marriage should be and
The rest of us regarded it with
Envy and despair.

She always called him lover and
He always called her baby and
She always praised his brillance and
He always praised her wit.
No wife was more adoring and
No husband more devoted and
The rest of us were jealous I'm
Embarrassed to admit.

He always called her dearest and
She always called him darling and
He always hugged and kissed her and
She always held him tight.
They just announced they're filing for
Divorce tommorow morning and
The news has filled the rest of us with
Absolute delight.

Were "He" and "She playing to the grandstand? What were "The rest
of us " hooked into? What do you think they were telling themselves
about their own marriages? If they thought "His and Her" marriage was
so great, what should they have been doing about their own marriages?
How could they have escaped the envy-jealouay-hostility trap?

100

Chapter Ten

IMPLEMENTING KEY 3 EXERCISES

Recognize - analyze - strategize - act. That's the path to taking back and building inner power and control.

STEP 1 - Gain perspective. IC is a very broad and basic area with many ramifications. Do an honest assessment across your life, roles, and daily activities. Target those areas of strength and those which you wish to develop more.It's a fact in social science that the process of observation itself changes that which is being observed. Thus, just becoming aware of an issue can start a chain of positive growth.

STEP 2 - Become more aware of your own feelings and reactions. Get in touch with your gut reactions and what feelings and thoughts trigger them. Identify your hot buttons. Catch yourself at the point your mood changes and ask yourself what's going on. Many of us, men especially, have a hard time identifying feelings, in part because we have a sparse "feeling vocabulary". Appendix 2 lists feelings words which can help you increase your precision at doing this.

STEP 3 - Control your self-talk. We give more power away by worry, "I can't", and other negative self-talk than by any actions we do. Language conditions us. What we tell ourselves determines our emotional state, our perceived level of our power, and subsequently our actions. The exercises that follow will help you reframe and recondition your thinking toward freedom and flexibility. They will help you to develop greater positive assertiveness.

(1)   **Be careful how you use "I am"**. The words, "I am" describe your essence, **you, your permanent qualities**. Whatever you say after "I am" labels you in your own mind. Use "I am" liberally to describe your strengths and positive qualities. Never use it with negative labels.

Describe your actions in behavioral terms: doing, thinking, feeling, etc. saying "I didn't think..." is more positive (and realistic) than, "I'm stupid...". Besides, no one act can adequately label a whole person anyway.

(2)   **Dispute negative self-talk**. Challenge in your mind any overgeneralized negative assumptions or self-statements. Use reason, reality and truth. Debate with yourself, if necessary. Refuse to awfulize, catastrophize, or overly exaggerate negative past, present, or future outcomes. Avoid absolutist thinking; "never" or "always", when describing your situation.

(3)   **Practice thought-stopping**. This helps cut out the chain of worry, obsessive thoughts, and automatic chatter that goes on in our brains. When negative thoughts occur, picture a big red stop sign before your eyes, say "STOP", and shift your mind to positive or neutral topics. You may have to repeat this frequently in the beginning. Be persistent. It works wonders. By so doing, you are training your subconscious mind to bring up more positive thoughts and images.

(4)   **Don't jump to conclusions**. When "crap" happens, suspend immediate judgment. Take time to sort out the real impact. Refuse to be overwhelmed, to over-generalize or over-react. Gain emotional distance. Break big situations down into manageable parts. Find positives behind apparent negatives. (This last suggestion is a Key 4 issue. Key 4 exercises will also help you build on Key 3.)

(5)   **Resist negative impulses**. Listen to your conscience. Buy time before acting. The old advice of counting to ten works wonders, so does a cold shower, or shifting gears and doing something else.

(6)   **Focus on solutions, not problems**. Problems are really veiled opportunities for growth and action. Focus on what you **can do**. When one focuses on what one can't do, he usually stops there, quits or "resigns himself to his fate". When things go wrong, don't muck around brooding over mistakes. Rather, look for actions that you think will work the next time.

(7)   **Never give up. But don't beat a dead horse either.** Sometimes the best solutions aren't readily apparent at the outset. Yet, if no solution is forthcoming, move on. Don't let yourself go down with **any** ship!

(8)   **Use the three magic words.** There are three sets of magic words, one or more of which can appropriately crush most of our negative self-talk.
"This too shall pass."
"Consider the source."
"So what!"

These help you gain perspective. When a difficult situation occurs that could lead you to ruminate or worry, try using one or more of them, backing them up with logic and reason. Then take appropriate action.

(9)   **Stop comparing yourself to others.** There is one exception, however. Compare only to learn and improve, never to judge the worth of people. If I observe you performing better than I, rather than lapsing into jealousy, anger or despair, I would do better to study what you're doing to determine how I could improve. Of course, you want to avoid being a copy-cat.

(10)   **Identify and develop your positive uniqueness.** Look carefully at your personal blend of skills, assets, limitations and personality. Note how personal past experiences have contributed to where you are today. Describe your unique style in terms of a few key positive phrases such as "I'm humorous, imaginative. I always see

the big picture", or "I'm a pensive thinker who brings depth to any discussion", or "I'm the life of any party."

Once you identify your uniqueness, celebrate and love it.

A hint: Unique doesn't mean "the only one in the world who___." There are many comedians, for example. There is only one Bill Cosby. What he does isn't unique, **how** he does it is.

(11)　**Don't imitate, innovate.** Develop your own unique creative style and potential. Reinforce Key 2.

(12)　**See yourself as an ACE:** an Active Creator of Events. Refute victim thinking and helplessness. Actively visualize yourself as a causal agent - one who makes things happen, who directs outcomes, who takes full personal responsibility - then take charge!

Act confidently, even if you're not. "Whistle a happy tune" and fake it till you make it. By doing so, you raise your confidence bar. Remember the impact of imagination on your subconscious!

(13)　**Manage Your Anger.** Refuse . . . to be intimidated . . . to act with hostility . . . to be desperate . . . to play tit-for-tat or get even . . . to get hooked into fighting or useless competing . . . to hold a grudge . . . to base your moods on external events . . . to let one big issue such as trauma, abuse, or handicap become the defining characteristic of your identity, self-esteem, or relationships...to blame others. All of these waste your energy. They hand off your power and leave you feeling weaker and dissatisfied. Start with your self-talk. Ask yourself, "Is it worth spending my energy on this? How can I improve the situation? What's the best use of my mind, time and talent?"

(14) **Shrink intimidating people down to size.** Not by hurting them back, but by refusing to get hooked. Many chronically "difficult" people have their own problems and are hurting inside. Most are not as formidable as they appear. Recognizing that fact can help. While they control their behavior, **you** control their effect on you. Detach emotionally as best you can. Use their actions as an opportunity to show grace under fire and be a bigger person by rising above pettiness. Don't dwell on those people. Key 4 exercises will help here, as will the Mental Training Exercises which follow.

(15) **Don't create contests where they were never meant to be.** Don't compete when you don't need to. Choose your battles wisely. **You** decide whether you'll get involved.

(16) **Let go of envy, jealousy and hostility.** Take your eyes off of others and focus on yourself. Mind your own business and count your own blessings.

(17)   **Turn envy into a springboard**. First ask, is what I envy in others really right for me as well? If not, let it go. If so, then set your own goals and put your energy into attaining those. Live and let live.

(18)   **Redefine "success" in your own terms**, away from society's or others' standards. Include quality of life in your definition, not just money. Set your goals in line with your own true needs and desires. March to your own drumbeat; set your own course and follow it. (But be careful not to rebel just for the sake of being oppositional.)

(19)   **Keep good company**. Associate with uplifting, positive, self-directed people who can inspire you and keep you on your toes. If most of your friends are aimless, lethargic, or negative, they may be undercutting your growth. If so, consider new playmates and playgrounds.

(20)   **Forgive and move on**. Forgiving others' transgressions is easier said than done. It also truly empowers you to demonstrate grace under fire and to rise above the situation. Retained hostility and rumination are testimony to our own impotent rage and perceived inability to take charge and change our situation. It imprisons us in our past, and gives past events excessive power over our present. Forgiveness isn't forgetting, it's coming to terms emotionally with the transgressor.

(21)   **Be, in your own way, the positive qualities
you most admire**. Why try to keep up with the Joneses
when you can be your own Jones? **Be the example for
others to follow**. An ancient Zen monk said, "Do not seek
to follow in the footsteps of the men of old. Seek what they
sought."

This is the capstone, the outworking of the first
three Keys. Does this mean you have to be super-saint,
super-human? No way. Larger than life isn't real; a fully
meaningful life is. Whether you're very visible or very
quiet matters not. **To be on the right track and to know it
- that's power**.

That's also influence. Think about it.

AFFIRMATIONS FOR KEY 3

I call my own shots.
I exhibit admirable qualities in all that I do.
I'm my own person.
The buck stops here.
I take full responsibility for my own thoughts, words and
       deeds.
I'm decisive - no excuses.
I soar to the stratosphere of my own uniqueness.
I'm wonderfully unique.
I love, value and cherish myself in positive healthy ways.
I'm open to others and am still my own boss.
I let go of envy, jealousy and anger.
I'm a person of power and peace.

108

I forgive all who wronged me and move forward in
firmness and love.
I let go of past problems.
I'm in full control of me.

VISUALIZATIONS FOR KEY 3

1. Close your eyes and relax. Picture yourself up in the
top row of a stadium looking down upon the stressful
activities going on around you as if they're happening
on the playing field. Exaggerate them, speed them up,
or in other ways add humor. See yourself as detached,
an onlooker rather than a participant.
2. Visualize yourself in a situation in which you used
to get hooked, angry, jealous, etc. See yourself handling
that situation with full emotional control and
detachment. See yourself demonstrating positive grace
under fire, managing the situation so that you remain
free and self-controlled, with a good outcome for all
concerned.

GET PROFESSIONAL HELP IF YOU NEED IT.

Some Key 3 difficulties are deeply ingrained, such
as habits, hostility, addictions, mental health problems or
some abuse situations. High IC folks do a lot for
themselves, yet they also know when "doing it by myself"
is counterproductive. They feel free to make liberal use of
professional resources and support groups when they may
be in over their heads, or when such help can speed their
growth.

FINAL THOUGHTS

"When is a person a free agent? When has he a free mind? You are free the moment you do not look outside yourself for someone to solve your problems. You will know . . . and feel free inside yourself when you no longer blame anyone, or anything, not even yourself, for unhappiness. You will know you are free because you accept life as the postman accepts the weather: he just walks his rounds and does not make a problem out of it." (1)

Willard & Marguerite Beecher

"Trust Allah, but tie your camel."

Islamic Proverb

A brief story:

Two Buddhist monks were walking along a soggy, muddy road in a rainstorm. They spied a young richly dressed woman standing on the corner. The older monk picked her up and carried her across the road to the opposite corner. At evening, when the monks arrived at the temple, the younger said to the older, "You picked up that young girl this afternoon. Don't you know as monks we can't touch a woman? It's dangerous." The older replied, "I put her down on the other corner. You are still carrying her." (2)

Key 4

**"HOPE is the fuel that propels us forward.
Indeed, no endeavor was ever undertaken without it."**

H.A.Olson

**We understand and respond to events,
not as they are, but as we have** labeled them.
Events are as we decide **they will be.**

H.A.Olson

**"Life will give you either a victory or a lesson.
Either way, you win."**
David Sandler, Creator, Sandler Selling System

**"Nothing in life is to be feared. It is only to be
understood."**
Patric Walker

"There are no crises, only transitions"
Edith Eva Eger

**"Your greatest worry can spur you on to your greatest
achievement."**
Art Linkletter

"Opportunities in life come by creation, not by chance."
Paramahansa Yogananda

111

Chapter Eleven

KEY 4

WORLDVIEW
"See Value and Opportunity Everywhere"

Energy begins with **perception**. So do opportunity and visionary thinking.

Try this exercise with a friend. Stand erect, feet about a foot apart. Extend your right arm straight out to your side, parallel to the floor. Your friend's task is to take your wrist and try to pull your arm down while you provide resistance. This isn't a struggle, but just to test muscle tonus. Do this three times.

First - think about a time when you were on top of the world; you felt like a real winner. When you have that time in mind, ask your friend to "test", to pull your arm down. Feel the degree of your resistance, your energy level.

Second - think now about a sad time in your life. With that image in mind, ask your friend to "test". Feel your energy level and degree of resistance now.

Finally - clear the sad image and go back to the original scene and winning feeling. "Test" again and notice your degree of resistance now. How quickly did your energy return? Reflect a moment on what you learned from this exercise.

You can't change what you can't see. You can't capitalize on it, either. But the power of Key 4 plumbs much deeper. Your **power** to create change, to break free of self-limitation, and to capitalize upon what comes your way is **directly fueled or limited by your outlook**, your world view. **What you see IS what you get.**

That's the point of the exercise. That's also why those caught in the cycle of depression, worry and EC often find it so hard to overcome. Negative thinking saps energy, both mentally and physically. Their outlook is constricted. They have developed, in effect, emotional tunnel vision.

"Empowerment" and inner strength rest upon a two-fold foundation: a heightened sense of one's own power (Keys 2 & 3) and an expanded, positive world-view (Key 4). Without these keys in place, full effective action is impossible. **You can't maximally succeed if you're afraid of failure, or doubt the value of the outcome.**

SCARCITY VS ABUNDANCE THINKING

If your motto is "the best things in life are scarce", you're more likely to think of life as a zero-sum game: if you win, I lose. You may scramble for existing finite resources and opportunities. You may be tempted to overly compete or undercut others, feeling that there isn't enough to go around.

The scarcity mindset fuels complaining, whining, envy, jealousy, invidious comparison, hostility and self-protection. It's a royal road to external control. In short, scarcity thinking promotes three reactive attitude/actions: compete and struggle to win, quit, or stay put and be satisfied with less. In each of these, energy and resources are misdirected and underutilized. Scarcity thinking also makes people more vulnerable to Key 2 ego issues and fears. **The biggest barrier posed by scarcity thinking is not lack of knowledge, but lack of vision.**

THE POWER OF ABUNDANCE THINKING

Abundance thinking is more than just optimism. It is a broader, deeper way of comprehending and coping with life. It sees a world of possibility, without walls or limits. It views everything in process - in a state of growing and becoming - rather than being static. While scarcity sees separateness and divisions, abundance sees connections, system and wholeness - even when such connections may not be readily apparent. Abundance also focuses on what one has, not on what one lacks. It is a critical building block for your self-esteem and positive relations with others.

WHAT ABOUT "REALITY"?

Most of us **really** use the term "reality" to connote limits, problems, and what "is". It becomes our fence. Embedded in this usage is a fundamental error: that what "is", is all there is. That notion is actually **selective perception**, excluding much more than it includes.

True reality is so broad, multifaceted, and interconnected that we cannot fully comprehend it. It includes both the tangible physical realm as well as energy and spiritual forces. Obviously we can only deal with small fragments of it at any one time. **Which** fragments we choose to perceive and deal with, however, is critical to our outcomes.

Abundance peers into the future, seeing long-term outcomes, solutions, benefits. Therefore, while whatever happens now may be critical, it is never final. Its view is also broad and wide. If one path doesn't lead to success, it finds another. Rather than scrambling for existing crumbs, abundance bakes a bigger pie. Abundance never quits. It provides staying power. Scarcity often sees faith and hope as antithetical to current reality, clouding one's view of reality. Abundance sees hope and faith **as** current reality, **clarifying** one's view of it.

Abundance redefines problems as opportunities and challenges to improve. It sees value and opportunity everywhere, in everything and in everyone. Thus, it energizes, excites, reduces fear, and builds courage.

TRAITS OF ABUNDANCE THINKERS

We each experience the abundance mindset very individualistically and personally. Yet to varying degrees, the following traits and outlooks would characterize most abundance thinkers:

- Abundance thinking as a **habit of mind.** It's how they **routinely** process their experiences.
- Optimistic, high on hope and faith.
- Feel deserving of life's good things.
- Curious and experimental, having a positive "what would happen if " outlook.
- More creative and innovative - visionary thinking.
- Sense of ultimate meaning and purpose to life, that there are no accidents, that everything happens for a purpose which we may discover and learn from.
- Attitude of expectation. Benefits will come; if not today, then tomorrow. Today's actions have meaning and possibility even though I perceive no direct reward at this time.

- Multidimensional, balanced sense of their own well-being. When evaluating how well-off they are,they include family, social, physical, financial, spiritual, talents, drive, etc. If they suffer loss in one area, e.g. illness or financial loss, they see positives in other areas that can compensate and renew their motivation.

- More prosperity-conscious, financial and otherwise. ("Prosperity" is not just monetary. It includes "wealth"in the above areas of family, etc., and overall quality of life.)

- High stick-to-itiveness, resilience.

CAREER IMPACT

Studies have shown that abundance thinkers more often do better in school, win at sports, are elected to office, are richer and have more successful careers.

Does abundance thinking impact the bottom line? You bet! In 1983, MetLife, concerned about sales force turnover, tested its new sales hires for optimism. A year later, twice as many pessimists as optimists had quit. After two years, optimists outsold pessimists by 31%. In 1987, MetLife began requiring all sales applicants to score high on an optimism test. Over the next four years MetLife increased its personal insurance market share by 50%. (1)

HANDLING ADVERSITY

Abundance thinkers have no magic shield to protect them from harm. Yet their ability to bounce back - both physically and emotionally - is aided considerably by how they view what happened to them.

Actor Christopher Reeve, commenting about the accident that paralyzed him, said, "Yes, it was terrible, but why should I be exempt? I had one very unlucky and unpredictable moment. The choice is whether to wallow in self-pity and musings about the past or to take a proactive stance about the future." (2)

Nobody wants adversity or tragedy, such as serious illness, hurricane or a major airline crash, but they are part of "reality". Yet, such events force us to choose - to give up and live with regret, or move on and create something new. Tragedy can bring out our worst or our best. We can't always control what happens to us, but we're totally in charge of our response.

Abundance thinkers may mourn a loss, experience anger and despair, but ultimately they **choose to find value and opportunity for growth** within the tragedy. They can **redefine** such experiences into challenges, using them as vehicles for developing greater strength and character, Vs feeling like an ongoing victim.

TURNING TRAGEDY INTO GOOD

Ten years ago, Clementine Barfield's son was shot while walking home from school in Detroit. Grieved and outraged, she formed SOSAD, Save Our Sons and Daughters, dedicated to wiping out violent crime in the city. She stated that her son had wanted to become a minister, and that this is now his ministry. "Your choice is to give up or go on. I chose to go on." (3) Other survivors have obtained legislation in support of their causes, changing the system.

Used properly, **tragedy galvanizes the survivors**, making our lives stronger and fuller, spurring greater accomplishment than might otherwise have occurred. This brings new meaning and purpose into events that would otherwise be senseless. Sometimes the greatest outcomes have come as a result of doors closed rather than doors opened.

The shock of tragedy is that it can instantly become all-consuming, canceling our view of everything else. We risk getting stuck in that mindset. While shock is natural, abundance thinkers see beyond and around current circumstances. They see the tragedy as limited, ultimately as a tiny blip on the big radar screen of existence.

While pain in life is inevitable, misery is optional. St. Paul, writing from death row, admonished people to rejoice in their suffering. What do you think he meant?

119

DIFFICULT PEOPLE AND ENVIRONMENTS

If you can't escape them, learn from them. Everyone we meet in life is our teacher. It's amazing how few enemies we have when we stop putting others into that role. Edmund Burke summed it up so well: "He who wrestles with us strengthens our nerve and sharpens our skill. Our antagonist is our helper." This attitude empowers us to be gracious and forgiving, and to take back our own power relative to those difficult people around us.

How to cope with a bad environment? Don't just sit still and "hope" things will change. Positively apply your Keys 1-4 skills, proactively striving for significance in your own area. Learn and grow, strengthen yourself. Refuse to be intimidated. Rise above. If things don't improve, refuse to be powerless. Strategize your options.

Abundance thinking ties hope to action, leading to activism for positive change, growth and well being. The greatest innovations and successes have often come as the result of barriers in the status quo. Just ask John Adams or George Washington!

FINAL THOUGHTS
A warning about "HOPE"

"Hope" is the first word in the opening quote for Key 4. Hope in that sense motivates us onward. Yet hope can be misused. Hope in the service of fear can become a **substitute** for action. When that happens, hope becomes the hope of the hopeless, a trap.

Beecher and Beecher called hope "merely wishful thinking, or a longing for Santa Claus to bail us out. Hope entices us to postpone living in the present, as if there were a future on which we could depend . . . . . hope is the fear of the present." (4)

"Of all sad words of tongue or pen,
the saddest are these - it might have been."
Author unknown

Hope should propel us, not lull us into passivity. **Hope** for your future; **live** in your present. **Hope AND Act!**

Chapter Twelve

IMPLEMENTING KEY 4 EXERCISES

The first steps in seizing opportunity are (A) to **actively seek opportunity** in old and new places, and (B) **expect to find it**. Daily develop and fine-tune your openness to possibility and prosperity. This may mean overturning prior self-limiting patterns and beliefs.

"Abundance" has been dissected in the last chapter. Rate where you stand on each of those aspects and then consciously strive to think in those terms.

New habits of thought derive either from a life-changing overwhelming experience, and/or from daily diligence: catching, challenging, and correcting the old thoughts as they occur, and **coaching yourself to think differently**. The exercises for Key 3 followed the same vein and serve as a foundation for Key 4.

REFRAMING

The overriding exercise and skill for Keys 3 & 4 is "reframing" - consciously looking at existing events in new ways, creating new meanings and interpretations to what we experience.

When I reframe a "problem" as an "opportunity", my whole perspective changes. So do my feelings. I may no longer fear it. I may even become excited and energized about it. I open incredible new vistas for understanding and possibility. All of the following exercises involve some degree of "reframing".

(1)   **Recognize that you deserve to succeed and prosper**. Many self-critical or perfectionistic folks don't feel they have a right to success because of past sins, failures, whatever. Success is not a reward - nor is failure a punishment - for living a good or bad life. They are strictly the result of activities and mindset. If you feel you deserve to succeed, you will. If you don't, you will subconsciously set limits on what you allow yourself to achieve. You may stop short of your potential. (Remember Will VS Imagination?) The words **"Hopefully** I'll succeed" often reflect self-doubt. Rather, say **"Naturally** I'll succeed." Then visualize yourself succeeding.

(2)   **Develop optimism: develop a positive explanatory style**. Dr. Martin Seligman (1) found that Explanatory Style was a prime differentiating factor between people who bounce back from adversity and succeed at higher levels and those who did not. Seligman cites three critical dimensions to explanatory style:

> **Permanence**: whether good or bad events are permanent or temporary.
> **Pervasiveness**: whether good or bad events are situation-specific to the point of our lives at which they occur, or universal, spilling over into other areas.

Personalization: Who is responsible when good or bad events happen: me (internal) or others/ circumstances (external).

Optimists see setbacks as temporary, such as bad luck or ill preparation, and good events as the result of abiding internal causal traits such as talent, skills and personality. Pessimists see the reverse - bad events are the result of permanent or ongoing conditions ("I'm no good at this"), and good events as temporary ("I was lucky this time"). Those who see success as temporary may quit after a big success, figuring they may not be as lucky next time.

Optimists view setbacks as limited. If I fail at an important task, my life can still go on without serious interruption. **Positive events are seen as the result of ongoing causes** ("I'm clever and bright"). Pessimists see the reverse - setbacks spill over into the rest of their lives or are characteristic of their total selves ("I'm stupid", or "I'm a failure"). Successes are viewed as limited in scope and duration. They tend to catastrophise or overgeneralize negative events, so that when one area of their lives is hurt, every aspect suffers.

Pessimists excessively blame themselves for their failures and harbor feelings of low self worth. **Optimists more readily see the role of external events** and other mitigating factors in the problems they face, although they accept appropriate responsibility. **They see internal qualities such as talent and skill as causal for good**

125

events. Thus they trust themselves more to succeed in the future. By now you can see how Explanatory Style also sets us up for Internal or External control.

Now for an example. Suppose you bombed a big presentation at work. The pessimist might say, "Boy, I'm really shot. They'll never trust me with a presentation again (permanent). I'm a real flop (universal). I haven't got it, I guess. When I really have to perform, I can't cut it" (Internal, low self esteem).

The optimist might say, "I did a really poor job. I didn't prepare enough (temporary cause, changeable). Next time I'll prepare better. They didn't like this presentation, but I know they respect my work and my customers continue to buy from me, so I'll be OK (situation specific). I never had training in public speaking (external). Next time I'll get coaching."

Now how about a success of yours? Did you view it as typical of your capabilities, or write it off as luck? Did you view it as a fluke, or as repeatable?

Practice describing positive events in terms of lasting, abiding, or universal causal factors. Identify any positive skills or qualities of yours that contributed to it. Identify positive growth or learning in yourself that happened as a result.

Describe negative events in terms of temporary, situation specific causes. Identify external factors that contributed to the root outcome, but be careful not to fall into blaming or excuse-making. Look for positive opportunities and value that might be hidden within.

Often negative thoughts seem more powerful than positive ones. Usually our negative thoughts and fears are **highly specific**   ("I'll lose my job."), while positive thoughts are **vague** ("The sky is blue, all's right with the world."). Vague can't compete with specific. Make your positives as specific and impactful as you make your negatives.

(3)   **Look for positive purpose in your current circumstances,** Remember that "positive" and "negative", "good" and "bad" are relative terms. A "bad" experience could yield a "good" outcome.

Play with the notion that whatever your current circumstances, **you are in the right place at the right time**. If this were so, if there is a purpose for what you're going through, what might it be? What lessons are you supposed to learn and apply? Then seize the moment. **Act as if** you're in the right place at the right time. How can you fulfill your purpose? How can you enhance significance?

(4)   **Weave the fabric of your action and outcomes over time**. Review past successes. What did you do to achieve them? What opportunities did you seize or create? Also identify positive outside influences in your life from

childhood on. Notice any patterns, and how they contributed to your strengths.

Now do the same with adversities. How did you cope? Assess how they made you stronger. (Note: I'm not asking **whether** you're stronger, I'm **assuming** you are. **If you assume your strength, you will discover your strength**.)

(5)   **Develop your spirituality**. A spiritual sense adds meaning and purpose to life and is a tremendous comfort. "Spiritual" does not necessarily mean "religious", although for many, religion is how their spirituality is understood and expressed. Developing your spiritual side is a very individual issue. There are many directions you can take and resources available if you look for them. Don't be afraid to experiment if this is new to you. And don't be afraid to pray. That's one of the best resources there is, even if you're not "religious".

(6)   **Put yourself in the way of opportunity**. Get off the sidelines, into the mainstream. Get active and involved in networks that can open doors for you. Help others first, **then** they will help you.

(7)   **Identify and expect "meaningful coincidences" in your life**. A "meaningful coincidence" is something that comes to you, out of the blue, just when you need it. These have happened to me very often, and some have involved money.

Frequently I'd be working on a problem. During a break I'd pull a book "randomly" off the shelf and open it in the middle just to browse. Right on that page would be the info I needed. In other situations people would come into my life out of the blue, with just what I would need. Creating these is a focus issue. We'll deal with how to bring them on in Key 6. **Develop your attitude of positive expectation**.

(8)   When you wake up in the morning, before getting out of bed, **consciously determine the kind of day you're going to have**, in detail. Then visualize it happening just that way.

(9)   **Identify and capitalize upon your area of freedom**. Regardless of what your job or situation in life - regardless of policies, rules, procedures, limits, circumstances - there is still much you can control.

Look beyond job duties. Look for chances for leadership or activities that you see need to be done. If you look in the dusty corners of your job description, you may find a broad range for potential motion. Focus on what you **can** do or change, not on what you can't. Don't assume limits.

If you're heavily overworked, you might trade off some mundane duties for more interesting ones. Naturally this must be balanced with team or company needs. (This exercise is the place to begin if you want to reposition yourself within your current organization.)

129

Of course, **how** you do your job, and the attitude you bring to it, is **completely** up to you.

(10)   **Think, "ME, INC."** regardless of who writes your paycheck. Think of yourself as self-employed, your own boss within your area of freedom. As such, your task is to provide excellent service and be awarded future business.

At "ME, INC.", you are at once the boss, the staff, the product, and the marketing department. What decisions and actions can you take that will add value and open new windows of opportunity?

(11)   **Develop your creativity. Become a visionary thinker**. Creativity is not making something out of nothing. It is seeing connections between seemingly unrelated objects or events. Think systems and wholeness, not separateness. Look for connections and trends . . . . Don't just find a need and fill it, **imagine a need and create it**.

(12) How can you get the "market" to adapt to you, not you to the "market"? . . . . Track and log your creative ideas. You might need them later . . . Practice creative daydreaming and flights of fantasy around particular issues important to you. Write down your fantasies and results. While others focus on the donut, you look for the hole. Ask positive, "what would happen if..." questions and read cutting-edge literature. Take workshops to expand your visionary skills. Most of all, **define and imagine yourself as a visionary thinker**. That's the first step in raising your creative bar.

AFFIRMATIONS FOR KEY 4

I see value and opportunity everywhere.
I am completely creative.
I am a visionary thinker.
I routinely see what others miss.
I have immeasurable insight and wisdom.
I am a magnet, attracting opportunity (prosperity).
All my needs are being met.
I courageously seize opportunity.
I always expect and receive the best.
The world is my oyster.
"The force" (or "God" or "my Higher Power") is always with me.

(Create your own affirmations about specific opportunities, situations, or needs in your own life.)

VISUALIZATIONS FOR KEY 4

1.   Visionary thinker and problem solver. Imagine yourself in these terms. See yourself solving problems as if you had cutting edge or futuristic insight.

2.   "Hall of Greatness". Visualize yourself walking powerfully and confidently down a magnificent long hall, blocked with several passage doors. See them open before you one by one, permitting you to pass through. At the end, visualize yourself reaching an important goal.

131

3.   "Magnet for opportunity (prosperity)". Imagine good events   and opportunities being attracted by you and pulled toward you, sticking to you or falling into your lap. Do this scene for money and other needs. Play with this image. Have fun.

Introduction to Keys 5,6 & 7

ENERGY/ACTION

You have only so much energy. Where are you directing it?

We've come to a transition. Keys 1-4 focused on developing who and what you **are**. Now we're shifting gears toward what you **do**. You know quite a bit about **what** to do. The real issue is **how** to channel energy and action for peak performance.

The whole 8 Keys System is circular. Developing Keys 1-4 sets you up to best succeed with 5-8, which in turn strengthen 1-4.

Keys 5, 6, and 7 all deal with energy. In reality "energy" is a unitary concept. Separating it into three "Keys" is artificial, but it is done to highlight three prime aspects of energy liberation and use:

Key 5 - **Process**: How to "flow", accessing and using your peak performance state VS struggling with yourself and others.

Key 6 - **Focus**: Where to direct your energy for best results. Task, goals and the power of awareness are emphasized.

Key 7 - **Meaning of Activity**: Intrinsic VS extrinsic motivation, and how to get more joy and satisfaction and results from your daily activities.

There is some natural overlap in Keys 5-7. As you work on any one of these, you will be enhancing the other two, and you will be fulfilling in action what you have begun in Keys 1-4.

THE KEY TO DEVELOPING MASTERY IS ENERGY-MANAGEMENT - Let's begin!

"Where does the power come from
to see the race to the end?
It comes from within."
Eric Liddell

Key 5

"Never confuse activity with effectiveness."

H.A.Olson

"To compete well, you must play to win, but playing to win can turn into an obsession which deteriorates your ability to play to win. Play as if everything depends on the outcome, and then walk away as if nothing depends on the result."

Guy Kawasaki
Apple Computer

"Expect everything, demand nothing."

H.A.Olson

"Whatever you fight, will fight you back."

H.A.Olson

"In any contest between power and patience, bet on patience."

W. B. Prescott

"To win, you have to prepare to win."

John Avianantos

Chapter Thirteen

KEY 5
PROCESS

"STREAMLINE YOUR ENERGY"

Once when I was shark fishing, I had caught several 100+ pound sharks by midday. Then another boat with a camera crew sailed up next to us. It was the local news who had prearranged to do a documentary on shark fishing with our captain.

During the interview, another shark seized the bait. I grabbed the rod and brought the shark to the boat in about 20 minutes - of agony. My muscles were tight, I was tense. Normally I fish relaxed. What was different this time? The cameras were rolling during the entire episode!

In the quest for peak performance, streamlining your energy is essential. Basically it's a two-phase process: (1) achieving the Peak Performance State (the Zone), which athletes sometimes call "the winning feeling", or "being on a roll", and philosophers refer to as a state of "ecstasy", and (2) learning reliably how to get out of your own way.

THE LAW OF REVERSED EFFECT

Often when the pressure is on, we "clutch", we struggle with ourselves, with our internal demands, or with others (in my case, with the shark). It's common advice: when the goal is important, try hard, play hard.

The problem is that in "trying hard", usually we tense up and play brittly, both physically and mentally. We pressure ourselves with worry, perfectionism, and demands to win or excel that immeasurably add to the tension of the situation. When that happens, Bang! We've shot ourselves in the foot. We're more likely to err, or in physical activities, increase the risk of injury. We're also more susceptible to frustration and anger.

Coué's Law of Reversed Effect states that the harder we "try", the less likely we are to succeed. **The more an athlete pressures himself to win, the less likely he is to find his Zone.**

Why? Because what is required of the body/mind to access the Zone is **completely antithetical to "trying"**. Work and play relaxed, "smart, not hard". Serious effort is required for success. Often, "talent" is just hard work. The paradox lies in **how you go about applying effort**. That's the make-or-break factor.

Studies of athletes show that pros accomplish greater strength with less physical and mental effort than beginners. Part of the reason lies in conditioning and

137

practice and part is mental attitude. The 80-20 rule also applies: 20% of the effort yields 80% of the results.

ATTITUDE/ACTIONS THAT CREATE STRUGGLE

The following will lead you to struggle or fight: impatience...anger...putting pressure on yourself to succeed... fear of failure...needing to show off, look good or save face... worrying how your opponents are doing...exaggerating the importance of winning **this** contest or the negative consequences of losing. . . having to prove your worth . . . an overly competitive attitude. . . comparisons, etc. Notice how many of these are Keys 2 & 3 issues? **Nail Keys 2 & 3 and you're a leg-up already.**

The above traps are all **energy-disbursive**. They take your focus off the target, breaking your concentration (Key 6). This divides your energy and creates **anxiety**.

ANXIETY VS AROUSAL

Tension can have positive or negative aspects. Like a properly tuned violin string, the right amount produces a beautiful outcome. Too much or too little can undercut you. Many folks deny their tension, pretending it isn't there. They fear their tension because their tension ends in fear.

Peak Performers admit tension and learn how to manage it well.

Anxiety is rooted in self-doubt and fear. It can cause you to freeze up. If fear of shame gets involved, the problems described in Key 2 kick in. Anxiety can quickly arise if you see the demands of the situation (or "winning") as higher than your perceived skill or capability level.

Arousal is necessary. It is rooted in faith and optimism. Arousal is high motivation, excitement and desire. It's expressive, and produces tension akin to the race horse in the starting gate - psyched up and rarin' to go. Of course, even arousal can be overdone. The right amount, however, can be the royal road to the Zone.

THE PEAK PERFORMANCE STATE

You've been there. Probably many times. Maybe at work, or while performing an enjoyable task or hobby. Maybe in sports or play, or during a good conversation.

You felt exhilarated, a mountain-top experience. Mind and body were in total harmony, as if you went on autopilot. It all just happened, effortlessly. Everything clicked. Perhaps you outperformed your normal limits. You didn't have to think about what you were doing. You probably didn't "think" at all. You acted naturally, on instinct. No thoughts of past or future, winning or losing. No planning. You were totally focused on the task, totally absorbed in the present moment. Everything else was blocked out, ignored. Time seemed to either speed up or slow down - you weren't conscious of time because time didn't appear to matter. If there was physical pain, you didn't feel it. And when it was over, if someone asked you how you did so well, you probably couldn't tell them!

That's the Zone. It's a state of mindlessness that can occur during many types of activity. Many muscular and brain functions happen automatically to get you there. At the instant of peak performance, the brain's left hemisphere relaxes its planning and analyzing functions and the right hemisphere takes over. The left hemisphere erupts in a burst of alpha brain waves which relaxes tension. Endorphins are secreted which kill pain.

When you're in the Zone, you perform at your best. All of your skills and talents naturally come forth. No amount of "trying" can equal this experience.

The Zone seems to come to you willy-nilly, when **it** wants, seemingly independent of your needs or desires. You can't **force** yourself into your Zone, but you can **prepare** for it by setting up proper conditions for entry. You can also **trigger** it into action when you need it. The trick is in knowing how. As we shall see later, Will and Imagination are involved.

Think about occasions you were in your Zone, VS times when you wanted it but it eluded you. **What** was different?

CONDITIONS FOR PEAK PERFORMANCE

For over twenty years, Mihaly Csikszentmihalyi ("chick-sent-mi-high-ee") researched the Peak Performance State. He dubbed it "flow" and identified several conditions which increase the probability of entering the Zone or "Flow" in everyday life: [1]

- Having clear goals, rules or processes which require specific responses

- A challenge that will push you, yet lies within the realm of your capability. (Preferably a socially responsible challenge, not just excitement for excitement's sake.)

- An activity that provides a new complexity or opportunity for growth.

- Receiving feedback. You know how you're doing, you see results.

- Having an intrinsic interest in the activity itself, not just in the benefit you might receive.

- Focusing on the task itself, not on outcomes such as winning.

- Staying mentally in the present moment.

For flow to occur, you need to balance challenge and skill. High skill and low challenge leads to boredom or apathy; high challenge and low skill yields frustration or anxiety. Boredom never lets flow develop; anxiety kills it. Flow most often occurs at moments of "positive stretch", when your goals are above your head but within your reach. In the Zone, work and play blend, becoming indistinguishable.

Almost any physical, mental, or social activity can put you into the Zone **as long as the above conditions are met**. That's why it occurs so frequently while pursuing sports or hobbies, while so few people ever experience Flow while sitting around watching TV, or just engaging in small talk. Yet even repetitive tasks such as housecleaning or assembly line work can become flow experiences if you give them proper attention to detail, or make a challenge or game out of it.

While I was a kid, I hated to cut the lawn. I sometimes made it interesting by cutting geometric patterns in the grass, or clocking my time to see how quickly I could cut certain segments (and still do a nice job so Dad wouldn't yell!)

Entering "flow" also improves your self image. You sense increased internal control and self esteem.

TRUE MASTERY

There are four levels or stages of learning for any skill: (1) Unconscious Ignorance, (2) Conscious Ignorance, (3) Conscious Mastery, and (4) Unconscious Mastery - Peak Performance.

At stage (1), you don't know a given task, are unaware that the task exists or that you need to know it. At stage (2) you realize that you didn't know how to do the task. As you attempt to learn it, you reach stage (3), where you practice the task step by step, paying attention to the details required to do it properly. Then you reach stage (4), the stage of the subconscious feel of Peak Performance. You can do it in your sleep, without thinking. Even after reaching this stage, world class athletes and performers will return to stage (3) in practice, working to fine-hone specific skills so that they can accomplish them even better at stage (4) "when on stage". They also may revisit stage (2) when they discover some new aspect to their skill. The closer you get to stage (4), the greater likelihood of experiencing flow or entering the Zone. If you're willing to make the initial energy investment in skill learning and practice, the rewards can be great.

True mastery is transcendent. When you know the fundamentals and skills so well that you make the skill your own, you put the stamp of your own style on your performance, and redefine the skill. Bruce Lee knew karate so well that he did it without conforming to set moves and techniques. He was one with his sport. He just did what

143

came naturally, and flowed. A performance "looks easy" as a result of diligent practice.

CREATE MOMENTUM

The dictionary defines momentum as "the **force of motion** acquired by a moving body **as a result of continuing in motion**." In other words, it means getting on a roll and building a head of steam as you go. Think about a boulder rolling down a mountain, or the civil rights movement of the 1960's.

In physics, and in performance, momentum is a "flow" issue. As you continue to do something important to you, you become more involved, more invested, more energized, more excited. For example, we speak of a cause "gaining momentum" as more people join in.

Momentum is the result of action and involvement. You can't force it. It occurs naturally. Your action creates energy which feeds back into the "system" helping you **keep** energized and active. It gives your performance an extra edge. When momentum is high, it seems as if you're being swept along. This is especially true when others get involved and support your efforts. Momentum is your ally. It is critical to **sustaining** motivation and growth. Without it, it's easier to quit or fall behind.

The next chapter and Keys 6 & 7 will deal with creating the conditions of flow and building momentum in more detail. Now let's turn to how you can streamline your energy.

144

TRY THIS EXERCISE

With a friend present, stand upright, with your right arm straight out to your side, parallel to the floor. Try to resist as hard as you can as your friend tries to bend your arm at the elbow. Your friend should face your arm, pushing with his right hand on the inside of your elbow, while his left hand grasps your wrist and pulls forward. Do this, and pay attention to what occurs.

Now extend your right arm again. Stare at the knuckles of your right hand. Imagine that your arm is a solid bar of iron, encased in cement. Imagine the steel-gray molecules fusing. No human is powerful enough to bend such a bar. When you have that image in mind, tell your friend to "pull". He repeats the same move as before. Note the results, comparing your tension/effort level in both trials.

When **you** resist, you increase effort and tense everything. When you get out of your own way and **let your subconscious mind take over** you are "stronger", yet you experience less stress and actual effort. How can you relate this exercise experience with your important tasks and goals?

POWER VS CONTROL

Ever hear the old saw, "Yea, though I walk through the valley of the shadow of death I shall fear no evil. because I'm the strongest person in the valley"? This is true power.

The distinction between "power" and "control" is subtle, yet it impacts your energy availability. **"Power" is real, "control" is an illusion**.

Most of us concern ourselves with controlling other people and the events around us. We try to cajole or make people do what we want. Obviously, in families and organizations there needs to be rules, procedures and discipline for infractions.

The problem occurs at the emotional level, to the degree that **in order to feel secure, other people and events must go our way**. Insecure people get caught up in a cycle of energy misdirection. The more unsure they are of their own strength, the more they struggle or demand the outside world to conform to their desires. But this is always a losing battle: other people have minds of their own. Life events and circumstances often are as they are, quite independent of any one person's will. "Control freak" behavior is often a sign of consciously or subconsciously felt impotence. **The path of control and the path of happiness rarely cross**.

146

The truth is, the **only thing in life that we can control is our own thoughts, feelings and actions at the present moment.** Everything else lies outside of our span of control, even though we can influence much around us. Every breath I take is a gift from the Creator. I have no "guarantee" that I'll be alive to finish this sentence. Neither do you. Yet in order to function we must have plans and make assumptions regarding our futures.

It is always a mistake to base our well-being on an attempt to control the uncontrollable. Rather, the alternative is to become the "strongest person in the valley", not in any comparable sense, however. Nail Key 3. Direct your energy toward building your own inner power and strength. Those who are truly powerful are so "in control" of themselves that they have little emotional need to control others' actions. Because their faith is in themselves, they believe that they can handle what comes their way. They are free to trust, and have nothing to fear.

You can either fight the dragon or fill the void. The choice is yours.

LETTING GO - THE PATH TO INNER POWER

The essence of "letting go" is opening yourself to surprise, possibilities, new insights, and new alternatives. This is your only hope for entering the Zone or really maximizing your potential.

This means letting go of certain "shoulds" or "musts":

- The demands and judgment you place on others and the world.

- Demands for **specific** outcomes of your actions.

- Perfectionism or the notion of "one right way" of doing things.

- Unrealistic demands upon yourself, including the notion that you have to do it all, all by yourself.

- Demands that good situations remain permanent.

- Limiting preconceptions about ourselves and others.

- Burdens from your past.

Whatever you "demand", you set up as a condition for your own well-being. Many of our demands are "hidden", operating outside of conscious awareness.

How do you get in touch with hidden demands? Look at your reaction when they aren't met. For example, if you "demand" that the world treat you nicely, you won't notice anything as long as everyone around you complies. But if someone treats you rudely, you get bent out of shape, Bingo! Granted, it would be **nice** if everyone acted nicely.

148

It's quite another matter to **demand** niceness in order to remain calm inside.

Look at your reaction, then ask yourself what triggered it. Was it just someone else's behavior, or was it really that someone did what you didn't like? **Whenever** you feel upset, angry, or become judgmental, chances are someone, or "circumstances", violated one of your hidden demands.

Letting go of demands is central to "flexibility", "openness", "resilience". Having a lot of "shoulds" or "musts" fosters rigidity and dis-ease.

Expect everything - demand nothing. This sounds paradoxical, but it is very liberating. So often we cut ourselves off from opportunity by having preset conditions as to how our hopes and needs must be satisfied or by forcing others into our mold.

There is one caveat about letting go of demands: if someone close to you is doing truly intolerable behavior. If that person is unresponsive to you, you may need to take appropriate assertive action. Don't try to force him or her to change, but decide what **you** will do, and do it.

PATIENCE, ACCEPTANCE, CALMNESS

"God grant me the courage to change what I can, the serenity to accept what I can't change, and the wisdom to know the difference." So goes the Serenity Prayer.

So much of the pain and dis-ease we experience in life comes from our confusion about what we can and cannot control. Life is constant flow in motion. Nothing lasts. We can't stop progress nor freeze anything in a point in time. We can't speed life up, either.

"Letting go" is not a passive act. It is not quitting nor resignation. Nor is it surrender to the forces of evil. **It is an active process of shifting and centering**: shifting off the distractions and excess baggage that slow us down, and **zeroing in on what really counts**. It's maximum emotional and physical efficiency in the service of creating your desired outcome.

For example, if you are going to fight injustice, don't do so with hot-headed reactivity. Do so with cool-headed patience, using proper timing, mustering your support and resources before making your move. Don't alienate opponents. If at all possible, keep dialog open.

As you let go of your inner pressure, you will notice increased creativity, intuition and energy. Stress will be reduced. Your physical and mental health will improve as well. You will be more in harmony with yourself and with others.

You'll also move faster. Dawdling and procrastination are often signs of fear and self doubt and the first symptom of struggle. Letting go reduces these barriers.

On my desk I have several bricks, all smooth as glass. They were washed ashore on a New Jersey beach after decades on the ocean floor. They were made smooth by the constant current of water flowing around them, patiently, day after day, year after year.

Water accomplishes much more by flowing with and around than by crashing through. So will you.

Be a channel for the power that lies within you. Don't block your own energy with your demands, prejudices, misconceptions and fears. Rather than struggle with yourself or others to accomplish goals, let your goals and plans be a guide for your power to flow freely. When someone once asked Marshall Foch how he was able to win World War I, he supposedly replied, "By smoking by pipe, not getting excited, and reserving all my strength for the task at hand."

FINAL THOUGHTS

You can't "flow" if your main goal is to prove yourself.

The key to effective change management - Don't try to force the change; control yourself so well that you are flexible and confident in being able to respond to it and guide it.

Don't fight back. **Rise above.**

Your greatest power resides in gentleness.

Attempt to create harmony and synergy in all that you do.

Chapter Fourteen

IMPLEMENTING KEY 5 EXERCISES

Of all of the keys, 5 is perhaps the most experiential, and perhaps the least tangible. Maximizing Key 5 involves liberal practice of Mental Training skills, in tandem with other behavioral practices. You can't force the Zone. Therefore, **to succeed, you must prepare to succeed**. The exercises and practices listed below are geared to set you up for peak performance.

(1)   **Overlearn the fundamentals** of your job or craft. Most of us like to skip these and go on to more interesting stuff. Thus we often don't have a solid skill foundation. Yet, full self confidence and entering the Zone can only happen when you can **perform without thinking**.

Dissect your job and identify at least 5 fundamental required skills. Then rate your capability on each. Create and implement a skill-development plan to bring each one up to stage 4 mastery. Make this process interesting to you, like a hobby would be.

(2)   If you need to reach mastery on a specific skill or talent, **PRACTICE - PRACTICE - PRACTICE**. . . then practice some more. Pay attention to the small details. Being able to reliably access the Zone when you need to is the result of readiness, facilitated by diligent, focused effort. Set up a **realistic** practice schedule and stick to it.

153

Ten minutes a day accomplished beats 30 minutes a day "promised" but not done.

(3) **Discover Your Prime Productive Style.** Your Prime Productive Style is how you typically perform when you're producing at your peak. This is where you do your best job. Yet most of us don't know what that style is.

Look back over your last 5 peak productivity periods, identify any tendencies they had in common. Ask yourself: What happened? What triggered them? How did you accomplish your goals? What processes did you use? What key resources did you use? Notice any patterns in setting or location, time of day, trigger events, length of time involved, whether you were active or quiet, alone or with others.

When you identify your Prime Productive Style, try to recreate on your job, or elsewhere, the conditions that contributed to it.

(4) When you "outperform yourself" or do an exceptional job, **accept that performance as natural for you**, within an expanded range of your capability. Don't negate it or deny it. Rather, tell yourself that you're getting better, that your success is the result of increased skill and good preparation, etc. This prompts your subconscious to build it into your self image. It helps you recreate that level more frequently in the future. (Imagination sets the bar!) Remember, **you can never "outperform" yourself**. What you have done is raised the bar a notch.

(5)　**Build Momentum for excellent performance.** Don't flash and fizzle. So many projects start with a bang and shortly run out of steam. Here's how to get sustained results: (A) believe in and enjoy what you're doing, (B) strategize and pace activities so that each step builds on the one before, (C) set short-term or small-step mini-goals, perhaps for each work day, or practice period. Create short-term wins for yourself. For example, if you want to lose 50 pounds, it's easier losing 5 pounds ten times than 50 pounds once. (D) Let yourself enjoy the process and results. Maybe reward yourself in some way for accomplishing your goals.

(6)　**Streamline your time, life and space.** Prioritize, organize, simplify if necessary. Eliminate waste and clutter. You needn't be compulsive nor perfectionistic about this, but living or working in messy space or allowing yourself a chaotic schedule can promote feelings of being overwhelmed. It can sap your emotional energy without you being aware of it.

Pay attention to your daily activities and routines. Which promote positive energy and which don't? Which non-productive ones can you eliminate or trade off for more interesting ones? Time and energy-wasting activities creep in unrecognized. Periodically taking stock will help you to keep on track and maximize positive results.

A more radical way to streamline is to specifically clarify **what really counts in your life**, what gives you true meaning and satisfaction. Make that your top priority.

Strengthen those activities that support it, lessen or eliminate those activities that interfere with it. **Aim for internal harmony and synergy**. Eliminate internal discord. Get all your energy forces flowing in the same direction, if at all possible. Revisit Key 1, particularly reviewing your core values.

(7)   **Create the positive stretch** - build challenges into your daily activities. Aggressively look for ways to make your important tasks more interesting or productive. Explore creative or different approaches to them. Pay more attention to the skills and details required to do them at peak levels. Set private performance goals for yourself (See Key 6 for goal-setting tips.) Refuse to be bored.

(8)   **Develop your intuition**. Pay increased attention to your gut feelings and hunches. Learn to "read" them and see how accurate they are. Start checking them against "reality". Let yourself follow them more in making decisions. Many of us have limited or shut down intuition as a source of data, believing it to be "unscientific". Actually, intuition is there to guide us. Learn to trust and use it.

(9)   **Work & play relaxed**. "Relaxing" isn't just lying under a beach umbrella. Relaxation can be very active. Almost anything you can do, you can do with the absence of excess physical or mental tension. The Zone is the epitome of Active Relaxation, but you can be routinely relaxed.

You can't **make** yourself relax; you **let** yourself relax. When you're tense, try deep breathing, taking a break, shifting your attention to pleasant thoughts, or picturing relaxing images in your mind. The more you practice these and the Mental Training skills, the more relaxed you will become and remain.

(10)   **Discover and release your hidden demands.** Review the last 5 times you became upset. What or who triggered these upset feelings? Try to put into words what occurred that upset you, or complete the phase, "I could be happy if only . . ." Debate and release the "if only's". Tell yourself that you let them go, that your happiness or peace is in your own hands; that you are free from any dependence on _____, etc.   If this exercise points up positive, proactive action which you need to take, take it. Otherwise, drop your demands and move on. (I know. This is easier said than done. Most of us need to repeatedly catch ourselves and remind ourselves to let go. It gets easier with practice as you develop a more emotionally liberated self image.)

(11)   **Stop competing and struggling with yourself.** Many of us are harder on ourselves that we are on others. Many who say "I'm competing with myself" are actually beating themselves up if they don't succeed, are never satisfied with their performance, or berate their failures. "Competing with yourself" is actually a counter-productive notion. Competition implies an opponent. Why must your opponent be you? Set responsible performance targets and pursue them intensely if you wish, but quit "competing" or

pressuring yourself. Rather, love and accept yourself whatever the outcome. Consider mistakes or failures as steps which shorten your learning curve; you know what **not** to do next time! **Work and play smart and relaxed, not hard & tense.**

MENTAL TRAINING: TRIGGERING YOUR ZONE

You will soar on the wings of Imagination to heights which Will alone can never achieve.

The arm-bend exercise showed you how to accomplish more with less stress - by giving over the reigns to your creative subconscious and getting out of your own way. Don't struggle, flow.

Imagination cannot, however, make a silk purse out of a sow's ear. "Mental Training" cannot compensate for no talent, lack of skill, and failure to practice. Rather, it will enhance skills already in place. It can help you develop your capability faster and improve probability of success. It also can eliminate anxiety and give you an immediate energy boost at the critical moment.

Harry Emerson Fosdick said, "Hold a picture of yourself long and steady enough in your mind's eye, and you will be drawn toward it."

Before any performance, mentally rehearse. (1) Stop for a moment, close your eyes and relax with a few deep breaths. (2) Visualize yourself performing flawlessly in every detail. (3) Support that image with positive affirmations about handling specific details outrageously well, and absolutely and completely succeeding and reaching your goal. (4) Then give yourself a . . .

TRIGGER CUE . . .

To actually access your Zone when you want to. Whether it's a golf shot, a sales call, giving a speech, or whatever, the general technique is the same. The runner in Chapter 4 was trained to close his eyes and tell himself "go - go - go" to get an energy burst. A salesperson might say "When I pick up the phone . . . when I walk into my prospect's office. . . I instantly enter my Zone". Follow that with a brief verbal description and visual image of the desired performance. A student may say, "Whenever I open my books to study . . ."

Your trigger cue might also be a simple and universal act such as purposefully pressing your thumb and little finger together, telling yourself that whenever you do this you automatically enter your Zone.

The trick in making Trigger Cues work is to repeatedly condition them in advance. Go into a relaxed state. Visualize and describe your cue happening in the future: **"Whenever** I walk into my prospect's office . . ." or **"Whenever** I press my thumb and little finger together..." Tell yourself it will happen and visualize it happening. Keep incorporating trigger cues into your mental rehearsal until, and even after, they start working in "real life".

159

Trigger Cues are actually "post-hypnotic suggestions" which you give yourself. They shape your subconscious and become a "habit".

AFFIRMATIONS FOR KEY 5

I work relaxed, I play relaxed.
Easy does it.
I let go and flow.
I go with the flow.
I am cool, calm and collected.
I enter my Zone automatically, whenever I need to.
Stress (or insults or put-downs, or . . .) rolls off my back
    like water off the back of a duck.
I always do my absolute best at whatever is important to
    me.
I remain cool under fire.
I am gracious.
I let go of needless demands.
I live and let live.
I always have just the right energy level for what I need to
    do.
I have boundless energy.

VISUALIZATIONS FOR KEY 5

The steps for visualizing peak performance were spelled out above. Now for what to visualize. Depending on your needs, consider any of the following:

1. A specific act such as a specific sport performance, sales call, making a presentation, etc.
2. A preparation or practice session, e.g. for writing, see the thoughts and words coming effortlessly and flawlessly, in just the right order.
3. See yourself successfully doing any of the 11 exercises in the first section of this chapter.
4. Visualizing goals. See Key 6.

TIP: Don't crowd your mind with many visualizations. Pick one or two issues to focus on repeatedly until you see results. Don't forget your Trigger Cue if accessing your Zone is part of your imagery.

EXPERIMENT: Periodically play around with your images and methods till you find what works best for you. If you want more help with Mental Training, The Playbook will give you actual scripts for Trigger Cues and additional Mental Training aids.

FINAL THOUGHT

" 'Luck' graces an athlete who has been putting forth a maximum effort for a long time. In my experience the breakout performance happens almost by accident; an accident that comes about because the athlete has worked hard to put all the elements into place: practice, good equipment, good technique, and a proper attitude to make improvements." (1)

Dave Erickson
Champion Shooter

161

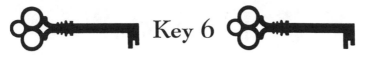 Key 6

"What you concentrate upon, you magnify."

H.A.Olson

"Keep the brain and conscience clear;
never be swayed."

Dwight D. Eisenhower

"How can you think and hit at the same time?"

Yogi Berra

"Maintain constancy of purpose"

W. Edwards Deming
(This is First of his "14 Points" for organizational transformation.)

"If you learn how to withdraw your attention from all
objects of distraction and place it upon
one object of concentration, you too will know how to
attract at will whatever you need."

Paramahansa Yogananda

"Truly peak performance can only happen
when you take yourself out of the equation."

H.A.Olson

163

Chapter Fifteen

KEY 6
FOCUS
"Keep Your Eye On The Ball"

G + D
F + D

Guts + Desire - They build motivation and release energy. Where is that energy directed?

Focus + Discipline is what brings your dreams into reality. Your ability to **focus** is your key to the Zone.

Focus is **"single-mindedness"**; it is the **total concentration of your energy** on one very specific thing. At the same time, it is **the avoidance of distractions**. When you're highly focused, you experience full sensory awareness, you are "in the moment". Shooting master, Brian Enos, says, "We can **think** our way through firing, but when we shoot there is no room for conscious thought. We shoot in the present tense." [1]

Key 6 takes Focus apart. We deal with what it is, how to develop it, and how to use it to propel you toward success.

KEEPING YOUR EYE ON THE BALL

Rod Laver tells potential tennis stars, "In concentrating you have to wipe everything out of your mind but the ball. Nothing but the ball. Glue your eyes on it. Marry it. Don't let it out of your sight. Never mind your opponent, the weather, or anything. Make that ball an obsession. If you can get yourself into that trance, pressure won't intrude. It's just you and the ball." [2]

Tennis coaches advise focusing so totally on the ball as it's coming over the net that you see the fuzz on it. Notice its spin and trajectory. Only then can you "know" best how to hit it to land where you want. (All of this without conscious thought). If at the moment the ball comes toward you, you're looking at your opponent or thinking about the score, you'll miss the ball.

Try this exercise. Hold your thumb at arm's distance up in front of you. Stare at your thumb so that it looks crystal clear. Now, without shifting focus, what does the wall in front of you look like? Now focus on the wall so that you see **it** clearly. Now your thumb looks fuzzy.

WHEN THE CHIPS ARE DOWN . . . .

Top athletes narrow their focus. They block out the score, the crowd, how they look to the fans, even the opponent. They tune in totally on their performance, on the process of the moment - nothing else, not even their goals. There's plenty of time for planning, strategizing and evaluating, but it's **NOT** when you're performing.

It requires intensive training to learn how to clear the mind and narrow one's focus. Fortunately, for our purposes, we don't need to narrow our concentration **quite** that much, but the same principles and benefits of narrowed and increased concentration apply.

AWARE VS SELF-AWARE

Concentration is not forcing your mind to think. That's **straining**. Nor is it thinking about a given topic. That's **contemplation**.

Concentration is being aware rather than self-aware. As the thumb exercise showed us, our focus and awareness can be placed **in only one direction at a time**. You're **either** tuned into what's going on around you **or** into yourself and your own thoughts, needs and interests. You can't do both simultaneously. Let's prove it: turn on the radio or TV, or tune into a conversation going on nearby. Give that your full attention for a few moments. Then shift your thoughts to a past success you had, or your next vacation, or whatever. What happened to your ability to recall the radio or TV program or the conversation while you were into your own thoughts?

When you concentrate undividedly on the task at hand you're **aware**. When you start to daydream or worry, you become **self-aware,** tuning out your surroundings. You haven't "lost focus", you've **shifted** it. You've become "distracted". What you actually did was "change your mind" to a new point of focus.

When I was a teenager, I sometimes read the lessons in church. When I read aloud, sometimes my mind would rush ahead of my voice and I'd stumble over words. One Sunday, I recall I was reading very smoothly. My mind was on my reading - I was aware. Midway through the passage, I thought about what would happen if my mind were to race ahead of my voice. At that instant, inadvertently I **shifted focus** to becoming self-aware. Now I was focused on slipping. And since **what you focus on, you magnify** . . . . you guessed it. I slipped up.

Incidentally, "self-awareness" as I've defined it is the root of "stage-fright" in all its forms, including social phobia. It feeds into the fear that often underlies win-lose competition.

"How I'm Doing" Vs "What I'm Doing"

When we're called upon to perform, the biggest temptation is to focus on **how** we're doing (evaluation). Because most of us are never far from thinking in comparisons, this is natural. Yet, focusing upon this issue can trip us up.

First, it's an ego issue. The ego takes your attention off the task and fixes it upon the self. It can lead to second-guessing, worry, and fear. Concerning yourself with the score, your relative standing, or whether your appearing or doing OK will boost inner tension. It automatically forces you to fight on two fronts simultaneously: (A) your current performance and (B) your outcome. Since you can't attend to both at once, your energy is divided. "How you're doing" also forces you into sensing whether you are above or below others, which reduces your sense of internal control. It can also lead to inconsistent performance (slacking off when ahead, pushing when behind). Thus, the "How" kills the "What". It shuts the door to the Zone.

But don't we all need to know how we're doing? Sure. That's just plain feedback and we need to take time to receive it: during practice or after performance, but **not** during performance itself, unless ongoing feedback is necessary to the **continuance** of the performance. Eg. a comedian needs to keep aware of audience reaction.

If you've nailed Key 2, it will be easier for you to be more aware Vs self-aware when the pressure's on. However, if the goal is to win a contest or beat an opponent, it's especially tempting to focus on him or her rather than upon yourself. This forces comparison.

Mohammad Ali knew this very well. Before a fight he would grossly berate and belittle his opponent. When the opponent got into the ring, all he could think about was Ali, about beating him. But who won? Anger increases motivation, but it decreases precision, misdirecting your focus.

The threat of evaluation has fascinating effects. It tends to interfere with the performance of higher skilled people, but can motivate those with lesser skills. Those with higher skills tend to be more intrinsically motivated, so evaluation is more of a distraction and interferes with the joy of performance. It also may hook the ego because higher skilled people may feel they have a reputation to lose if they slip up. Lesser skilled people may be more boosted by external motivation, which evaluation certainly is.[3]

When performing, focus on **what you're doing**, the task itself. Block everything else out. Any evaluation involved here is not one of relative personal worth, but what is the best way to proceed. The ego-flexible person uses feedback to see if her actions are properly directed and working, not to validate her worth. Since ego is on the back burner, she can accept criticism and advice as a useful improvement tool, not as a personal affront.

Are you more Task-Oriented or Ego-Oriented? See Box 15.1 at the end of the chapter.

To summarize:

Aware	Self-Aware
concentration	contemplation
in the moment	in own thoughts
ego-flexible	ego-invested
free of self-demands	controlled by
flexible	self-demands
	into should/shouldn't

Focus is tremendously powerful, but we've just scratched the surface. Let's go to the next level.

THE MAGNET PRINCIPLE

Whatever you focus upon intently or vividly imagine, you draw to yourself. Or as Harry Emerson Fosdick said in the last chapter, you are drawn to it. Either way, you increase the probability of its occurrence.

Paramahansa Yogananda put it this way, "By the power of concentration and meditation you can direct the inexhaustible power of your mind to accomplish what you desire and to guard the door against every failure . . . . if you learn how to place (your focus) upon one object of concentration you too will know how to attract at will whatever you need." [4]

Be careful! This principle can work negatively as well as positively. In 1978, aerialist Karl Wollenda fell to his death from a tightrope. Afterward, his wife stated that

170

for three months prior, all he could think about was falling. In the 1994 Winter Olympics, figure skater Brian Boitano did an aerial jump and spin, and fell upon landing. Later he said, "I've never thought this before. When I was up there, I suddenly didn't know how I was going to get down."

Here's the point: Be selective about what you focus on. **Imagine and focus upon success, not on failing or avoiding failure**. Your subconscious mind doesn't process the words "no" or "not". If you tell yourself, "don't fail", it will think about failing . . . . and since your subconscious' job is to bring what you imagine into reality . . . . Likewise, **focus on what you are for, not what you are against**. Look at yourself, your core values, your goals. Focusing on what you're against can distract you: focusing on your opponents or getting into negative comparative evaluations, can distract and undercut you. Negativity drains energy (Key 4).

There are several levels at which the Magnet Principle operates. The first is **heightened awareness**. Ever notice how, when you begin to think intently about a particular thing or topic, how many things or ideas related to it you begin to see? Think about the last car you bought. Around that time, I'd bet that you were amazed by how many more cars of that model there were on the road. There really weren't any more than usual; you just noticed them then. Before then, you didn't pay attention to them.

But could something else more powerful be operating? Parking in Cape May, NJ is horrendous in

171

summer. On one very hot summer mid afternoon, my family and I were driving to the beach. Not a parking spot was anywhere in sight. We all visualized finding a parking spot right where we wanted to go. We found one.

Coincidence? Perhaps. But when we succeeded 11 out of the 13 times we tried that image during that week, I'm not so sure.

SYNCHRONICITY

Psychiatrist Carl Jung coined the term "synchronicity" to describe "coincidences" that were connected so poignantly, that they couldn't have happened by chance. Quantum physics postulates that all things are connected, yet retain their unique attributes, as if there is a network or web that somehow envelops us all. Our selves, our thoughts - all are energy which exists beyond the bounds of the human body. For example, the "aura", or the energy field that surrounds the human body, has actually been photographed. Physics speaks of energy, metaphysics speaks of an intelligent creator or spiritual force. Religion speaks of God.

Call it what you will, you can probably recall meaningful coincidences. We introduced this idea in Key 4. That's the Power of Synchronicity: when I create an intention in my mind, I somehow put it out there into the universe. The more often I do it, and with greater intensity, - the more focused I am - the more likely for synchnonicity to occur. It's kind of like fishing: the more lines you have in the water, the more you'll catch. Religious people would see this as answers to prayer. That's also part of the reason this book is so heavy on affirmation and visualization.

Deepak Chopra, MD, considers the spirit a real force of energy, just as gravity and motion are. It is at the spirit level that we and the universe are all connected. He states, "connecting takes intention . . . . you can actually induce a synchronistic happening to occur when you introduce an intention at a subtle level of consciousness," [5] All of this to say that you can create an atmosphere that increases the probability of synchronistic happenings. Incidentally, Chopra has just defined "prayer".

Chopra outlines five steps to an intentional synchronistic experience: (1) accidentally or through meditation or silence, quiet your mind. (2) Nonverbally introduce an intention into that quiet space. (3) Get detached from the outcome. (4) Keep your ego out. (5) Don't force. Let the Universe handle the details. [6] The exercises in the next chapter will help you create synchronicity.

GOAL-FOCUS

The power of the Magnet Principle comes to full blossom when it comes to goal-setting. Goals are a powerful object of focus. As Goethe said, "When one is committed, providence moves too." Your subconscious can effortlessly assist your success . . . . provided you know where you're going.

173

Having goals is absolutely essential for maximum success in any endeavor. Goals compel energy and action, if they are effectively structured. Here's how. Make your goal:

- Emotionally compelling. You've got to want it badly, otherwise you won't invest your energy to making it happen.
- Personal, not competitive nor comparative.
- Totally positive.
- Outrageously wild, but doable. This can be a delicate balance. There is a difference between "wild" and "unrealistic". Wild goals incite creativity, excitement. Dare to dream. Many folks achieve less because their goals are too modest for their capabilities. Careful positive self-assessment is important.
- Highly specific and definable. State exactly what you want.
- Personally meaningful.
- Visual. Picture it or get/draw a picture of it.
- Time limited. Set long and short-range goals, with deadlines.
- Manageable. Break big goals down into parts. Celebrate your success when each part is met.
- Written. If you don't write it, you won't fulfill it.

AVOID GOAL TYRANNY

Goals are meant to be your guide and your energy channel, not your taskmaster. Don't pursue them so

174

relentlessly that other aspects of your life suffer or you burn out. Refuse to struggle. If you're struggling, there's something wrong with (1) the goal or (2) your approach. Check it out.

Be flexible. If needs or circumstances change, feel free to alter goals accordingly, but don't use this as a cop-out! If you fall short, don't punish yourself. Rather, realign your goals and move on. While a goal defines an outcome, you should have fun in the process of attaining it.

When you have set your goals, **act as if it is impossible to fail.**

To succeed, you must: **prepare** to succeed and **expect** to succeed.

WHEN TO FOCUS ON WHAT

In quiet times or breaks, in strategy sessions - focus on goals, plans, priorities. In actual practice or performance - only on doing the task itself. Goal-focus at that moment is a distraction. Remember, a goal is an outcome, while the task is process.

FINAL THOUGHTS ON GOAL-SETTING

While surveys report that 95% of the American population have no formal or written goals for their lives or careers, at some conscious or subconscious level, **all behavior is goal-directed**. There is no such thing as "no goals". Even our "accidental" behavior serves some inner purpose. Staying in one's comfort zone, maintaining the status quo is a goal at some level.

Therefore, the goal-setting task is not finding a new goal in the absence of goals, but a process of **changing** goals. This is important to recognize if you find yourself resisting a positive new goal. The new goal may be conflicting with an existing subconscious goal, such as remaining in the comfort zone.

The 8 Keys to Becoming Wildly Successful and Happy
BOX 15-1

THE EGO vs TASK-ORIENTED PERSON

Below are the characteristics of the ego- vs. the task-oriented person. Where do you fit on the task-ego dimension? To find out, fill out the scale below. Add up your score and divide by 10 to get your average score.

Task-Oriented	Points 1 2 3 4 5 6	Ego-Oriented
Asks "What must I do or use to solve the problem?"	- - - - - - - - - - -	Asks "Will I succeed or fail?" (often expects to fail)
Self-affirming, believes in self, confident	- - - - - - - - - - -	Self-questioning, doubt self, worries
Separates self-worth from performance	- - - - - - - - - - -	Identifies self-worth with performance
Accepts challenges, takes risks	- - - - - - - - - - -	Intimidated by challenges, avoids risks
Tries new activities enthusiastically	`	May limit self to what he or She can already do well
Takes responsibility	- - - - - - - - - - -	Rationalizes, makes excuses
Flexible, open-minded	- - - - - - - - - - -	Rigid, closed-mind
Cooperates, will share leadership	- - - - - - - - - - -	Must have own way, be the leader and/or call the shots
Creativity-oriented, looks for new ways and opportunities	- - - - - - - - - - -	Maintenance-oriented, protects What he/she has
Follows through	- - - - - - - - - - -	Often lacks follow-through

Average score of 2 or less = high task orientation. Average score of 5 or more = high ego orientation.

As you worked through this scale, you may have recognized certain traits in yourself that you have not previously put together into an organized whole. Hopefully this little scale has helped you to see more clearly your own "big picture." Only then can you most effectively determine where you are, what to strengthen, and what to improve.

Chapter Sixteen

IMPLEMENTING KEY 6 EXERCISES

We live in a world of soundbites. Distractions multiply. Demands compete for our attention. Life begins to approximate the Evening News: we jump from one unrelated story to another as we speed through our day. Surveys have shown that the average executive spends only 8 minutes on one project before moving to another.

This poses a dual problem: (1) **what** to focus upon, and (2) how to **sustain** focus. For most of us, this can often be quite difficult. This again raises the issue of **discipline**. While we have not raised that issue till now, all of the exercises and practices in this book have indirectly trained you in focus and discipline.

(1)   **Prioritize** - We hit this in Key 5; it bears repeating. Consciously take time to determine what is most important, what really counts. Carve out time to do this and review your priorities regularly. **Your goals always reflect your priorities**. That's why this is Step One.

Review Key 1. If you want success and happiness, cast your ultimate priorities in terms of Significance, what creates **value** - for your organization, your community, yourself.

ENHANCING & SUSTAINING FOCUS

(2)   **Practice keeping your eye on the ball.** This exercise is designed to help you improve concentration. Take a tennis ball, or maybe the palm of your hand, or some other common household object. Focus on it intently. Without using words, notice all of its properties: size, color, shape, texture. Move it, feel it, smell it, look at all sides. Do this for 3-5 minutes. If your attention wanders, gently bring it back. Notice how you feel upon completion.

Now take out an important project you've been working on. Go at it with the same single-mindedness. If distracting thoughts enter your mind, gently bring your mind back to the task at hand.

(3)   **Meditate daily.** Spend a few moments quieting your mind, or "going blank", or just letting yourself be open to whatever ideas come to mind. Do this in a comfortable chair with eyes closed.

(4)   **Targeted fantasy** - this could be combined with meditation. Let yourself relax. Then visualize yourself: (A) actually achieving goals, or (B) performing at your peak in some areas important to you.

Another twist to this technique is to let your fantasy run wild around the areas of your greatness, achievement, or talents and interest. You might visualize yourself in another age or place accomplishing great deeds, providing great service, etc. Wax creative and symbolic. Your subconscious will get the message.

SYNCHRONICITY

(5)   Develop your awareness and readiness for meaningful coincidences in your life. Look back over important positive or negative events or influences, achievements, or opportunities in your past. Reflect on what brought them to you or facilitated their occurrence. Often a significant opportunity is the result of a **chain of events**.

"A" comes into your life, which introduces you to "B", who facilitates "C" that enables you to carry out "D." I can trace some of my recent success to connections made 25 years ago, without which those recent successes couldn't have occurred. I have also seen how my life has turned in positive ways because of painful events and doors closed in my face.

Turning points, major trends or patterns may become apparent. You'll discover in retrospect connections that weren't apparent at the time.

The literature on synchronicity suggests that meaningful coincidences do not frequently occur to folks whose minds are closed to them. Are they just not on the lookout for opportunity,   or could it be that their close-mindedness shuts synchronicity down? Yet synchronicity happens quite often to those whose minds are open to possibility. Is that fact just a trick of perception, or is it **readiness**? I think it's the latter. If you're more open to opportunity, you are more able to recognize it and seize upon it when it occurs, and also to find the potential

181

positives in otherwise negative events.

Don't just look; train yourself to see. Repeat exercise 5 periodically, adding to and updating your perception of meaningful coincidences. Developing Key 4, enhancing focus, avoiding distractions, and doing Mental Training exercises - all help increase synchronous events. Perhaps the best way, however, is just to **expect them to occur**.

A caveat is in order here. Not every chance occurrence is a meaningful coincidence. The key is whether there is truly an underlying meaning or connection here. Does it come just at the right time for something important to happen in your life, etc.

GOAL-SETTING, GOAL GETTING

The last chapter outlined how to structure a goal. Now let's pick up where that discussion left off. There are several considerations that will affect your success:

(A)   Humans are more motivated by avoiding pain than getting gain. Explore the implications of achieving the goals you set. If there are **any significant downsides**, identify them and find a way to eliminate or negate them or turn them into positives. If you can't negate them, maybe you need to question if what you've chosen is the best goal for you. If as you move forward, you begin to lose enthusiasm, slip up, or in other ways resist, you may be experiencing "approach-avoidance conflict", wanting to have and desiring to escape the same thing. Identifying and dealing with downsides in the beginning will save trouble later. Most "resistance" is **goal-conflict.**

I once had a handsome client who wanted to lose 50 pounds so he could date girls. He started out well and then shut down at the 25-pound mark. As he got closer, he found that he was really afraid, not knowing how to act on a date. When he resolved that, he quickly lost the other 25 pounds.

(B)   Make sure that your goals are harmonious with each other. If you work on two goals simultaneously, and they pull you in different directions, you will struggle, and perhaps achieve neither.

(C)   Align personal career goals with your oganization's vision, mission and goals. You will perform better and more enthusiastically at work as a result.

(D)   Concentrate your energy. Shoot for only one or two major goals at any one time, in the area of your top priorities.

Now you're ready to write your goal. Many goal-setting systems exist. Here are two approaches to framing and programming it.

(1)   **Leave it to Providence**. State your goal as an affirmation. Repeat it and visualize it daily. Write it on cards, get or draw a picture of it. Look at it frequently. Then leave the details to your subconscious, and to the Universe. This method works well when you aren't sure of what you have to do to reach your goal.

A young man started writing out "checks fly into my mailbox" 50 times a day. During that time, as a sideline he'd been writing a weekly column for his small-town newspaper. One day a friend invited him to a party. He went reluctantly. At the party, he met a publisher who took interest in his articles and offered to publish them as an anthology. As the book sold, checks flew into his mailbox.

Now, would **you** be willing to try this, or do you doubt Providence's Power? We often don't get all we deserve because we don't trust the Powers That Be, both within and around us. Think about it.

(2)   **The Prophetic Affirmation** - I owe this one to Olympic gold medalist Lanny Bassham[1], although he uses a different name for it. Here's how it works: (A) **Write out your goal** in a few simple, powerful words. (B) **List the benefits** or payoffs you will receive when you reach the goal. (C) **List the steps** you will take to accomplish it. (D) **Set a date** by which you will reach the goal.

Now write the above on five 3x5 cards or large Post-It notes with the target date in the upper left-hand corner. (This is what you will see first when you look at

184

your cards.) Put one card in each of five key places, e.g. your bathroom mirror, your car dashboard or visor, your computer terminal or desk, etc. Whenever you go to that place and you see the card, stop and read it silently and flash a visual image of yourself achieving the goal. Lanny recommends doing this with only one or two goals at a time. Here's a sample:

10-31-97

(A)   I land 4 new accounts this month.

(B)   I add several thousand dollars to my income. I can buy a new car in three months. The family can go to Bermuda for the holidays.

(C)   I make 20 cold calls a day. I study up on closing skills. I consider objections as sales opportunities. I visualize closing a new account before each time I pick up the phone.
        I land four new accounts this month.

Notice that "visualizing" is part of the above action plan. Lanny guarantees that one of two things will happen: you will either reach your goal or stop doing your Prophetic Affirmation!

ADDITIONAL HELPS:

(1)   **Visualize yourself reaching your goal**; see yourself enjoying the benefits afterward. You also might visualize other important people in your life being proud of you, congratulating you.

(2)   **Break big or very long-term goals down into sequential sub-goals or steps in the process.** Visualize the final goal, then see yourself achieving each sub-goal. Mentally rehearse the steps you take at each level.

(3)   **Keep a progress journal.** Write down in your day-planner or elsewhere what you did each day toward achieving your goal. Also log whether you did your visualizations/affirmations. Don't get angry with yourself if you have empty pages some days. Rather, if you're not following through, look again at what you really want.

(4)   **Enlist others' support** in achieving business or professional goals. Share these goals with key colleagues. Keep personal or improved skill performance goals to yourself or share them just with your family or close friends, or your coach or mentor.

Goal-setting is a very personal issue. Go about it in your own way, but go about it. Keep it simple and direct. If you over-encumber yourself, you'll bog yourself down. Approached properly, you'll find Joy in the Journey . . . .

AFFIRMATIONS FOR KEY 6

When I'm doing something important to me, I'm totally
    focused.
My concentration is total and complete.
I'm totally focused upon _____.
I'm zealous for my goals.
I'm completely open to opportunity and leading of the
Creator.
What I truly need comes to me just when I need it.
I am a magnet for good events.
I am protected and cared for.
Goals come to my mind with complete clarity.

And, if you wish,

Checks fly into my mailbox.

(Visualizations for Key 6 have been included in the
exercises above.)

FINAL THOUGHT

"The moment one definitely commits oneself then
Providence moves too. All sorts of things occur to help that
would never otherwise have occurred. A whole stream of
events issues from the decision, raising in one's favor all
manner of unforeseen incidents, meetings, and material
assistance, which no man would have dreamed would come
his way."

- Goethe

Key 7

Success is not a destination. It's a journey."

Anonymous

**"True joy and happiness derive from meaning
and accomplishment, not from excitement
and entertainment."**

H.A.Olson

"I never did a day's work in my life. It was all fun."

Thomas Edison

"PASSION makes all the difference."

H.A.Olson

**"Play teaches the habits most needed for
intellectual growth."**

Bruno Bettelheim

**"Energy and fun: those are the keys to success.
Get that right - you win."**

Robert Townsend

**"Our society artificially separates play and work.
One it makes enticing yet trivial, the other
it makes burdensome yet necessary."**

H.A.Olson

189

Chapter Seventeen

KEY 7

MEANING OF ACTIVITY
"Find Joy In The Journey"

The sun beats down on the Arizona desert. Totally oblivious to the heat, the lone Navajo creates an intricate sand painting on the ground: vivid colors and timeless design, flawlessly executed. When he is done, he leaves. As the sun sets, the winds get stronger and the painting is blown into oblivion.

No matter. The Navajo had no thought of permanence. His heart and soul went into the process of painting. He connected with his heritage and his ancestors. He was one with his culture, the spirit world, and with the natural elements of sand and earth. He was in charge of his own actions. His mission was fulfilled.

Today we live in the disposable, microwavable plastic culture. We are results-oriented to a fault, often making process and relationships the servant of outcome. We look for speed, efficiency and the "quick fix". We often hesitate to do things unless we can be sure of the payoff: "WIIFM" What's In It For Me. In the process, we have truncated, and often lost, some of the key attributes that bode for true success, happiness, and, yes, even productivity. And now society and industry are just beginning to recognize what they are missing and are starting to scramble to regain it. Regain what? The Joy in the Journey - which ironically just may be the most important element to your "competitive edge".

The Joy in the Journey refers to **intrinsic motivation** and **process satisfaction**. That's a fancy way of describing sheer delight in doing a task for its own sake, not for any particular reward or outcome other than the satisfaction of a job well done. (Which, by the way, is much more crucial to "happiness" than salaries, rewards, bonuses or praise which, while important, quickly fade.)

THE ARTIST WORKER

Think back to when you engaged in a hobby or sheer play just for the fun of it. You didn't count time or energy. You gave it what it took. Maybe the "work" involved was meticulous, straining, or back-breaking, but you didn't care. Your focus was wrapped up in the task you were accomplishing. "Work" and "Play" became indistinguishable. You were directing your own activity. You were enjoying it. Perhaps you were in the Zone. In fact, experiencing Joy in the Journey is essential for reaching the Zone.

That's the quality of the Artist Worker or Athlete, who doggedly pursues the task out of innate interest and a desire to excel, quite apart from the outcome. The outcome may be important also, as it especially is for most tasks done on the job. But the **prime motivational driver** is the task itself, moreso than the reward. **Artist workers do what they love and love what they do.**

Teresa Amabile, studying creativity, discovered three basic ingredients in all creative work, from painting to executive decision-making. They are (1) expertise in the relevant field: talent, skill, information, (2) creativity skills: a work style characterized by concentration, flexibility, persistence, and openness to possibility, and (3) intrinsic motivation. The latter is the most important, but it has gotten the least attention.[1]   Czikszentmihalyi would agree.

WHAT FLOATS YOUR BOAT?

There are two categories of motivation: intrinsic and extrinsic. **Intrinsic motivation** comes, as we said, from the task itself. This is "pull" motivation. You are drawn to the task. Great effort may be involved in doing the task, but you accept that willingly. The task presents a challenge, the Positive Stretch (Key 5).

Intrinsic rewards include enjoyment, fascination, natural interest, opportunity for challenge, growth, learning, skill development, ability to direct and control one's own activities, sense of accomplshment, pride of craftsmanship, enhanced self-esteem, expanding or broadening one's horizons, and sense of contribution.

192

Extrinsic motivation is anything that drives you which is outside the task itself: contests, winning, rewards, medals, fame, glory, honor, recognition, acceptance, money, trade offs ("If I do this for you, you do this for me.") perks of any kind, following orders, pressure and threat of punishment. This is "push" motivation.

Notice that extrinsic motivators are usually **outcomes**. Extrisic motivation turns a task, or even a relationship, into **a means to an end**, as opposed to the task or relationship being an end in itself. This is a critical distinction for peak performance . . . and also for ethics, for other social issues, and for friendships: "Do you really like me or are you using me?"

In search of improving productivity, many firms spend inordinate time finessing and juggling the extrinsic motivators, hoping to find the magic combination to "turn on" employees. Such efforts are doomed to fall short of the mark.

As important as external motivators may be for us, **true motivation is intrinsic**. No one else can "motivate" you; you can only motivate yourself. The power of extrinsic motivators quickly evaporates. After all, how long will a person be happy to work for a given salary without a raise? Intrinsic motivation lasts, because it hooks and addresses what's important to you - your interests, needs, dreams - over the long haul. It needs no justification. Frequently when mountain climbers are asked why they do it, they respond, "because the mountain is there."

193

You want to get really turned on? Find Joy in the Journey. Make work and working and your other activities **personally meaningful**.

INTRINSIC VS. EXTRINSIC MOTIVATION AT WORK

Let's see how intrinsic vs. extrinsic motivation plays out. For example, an intrinsically motivated student enjoys the subject. He takes charge of his own studying. He works and practices hard, and does his homework without prodding by parents. Often he voluntarily goes beyond the requirements. Long after the test is over, he still knows the material and practices his new skills. Perhaps he continues to learn and fine-hone skills even more.

The strictly extrinsically motivated student is out for the grade, to show off, or to earn a reward from his parents. He takes the subject only because he has to, or to get an easy "A". He memorizes facts rather than taking the time to really understand and learn the subject's complexities. He does the least amount he can get by with, looks for shortcuts, and crams the night before the test. He is more likely to lean on classmates to do work for him. If his ethics are questionable, he may cheat or buy an "A" term paper rather than write his own. After the test, he quickly forgets what he learned, and when the course is over, he sells his books. Both of these students may pull "A's" but which would you rather teach or parent? Or have working for you?

PROCESS VS OUTCOME SATISFACTION

Related to motivation is process vs. outcome-oriented satisfaction. At what point do you get your main emotional payoffs? Many externally motivated persons, such as the swimmer in Chapter 4 or our student cited above wait to see whether the reward is great enough or if they won the contest before they determine if their preparation activities were meaningful or worthwhile. If they win, great. If they lose, outcome-oriented competitors may say it was all a waste. They may feel bitter at themselves for investing such effort in a "losing proposition". By suspending their judgment, so to speak, they rob themselves of the opportunity to allow their hearts and minds to get totally engaged in the preparation activities or the contest or performance itself. Their satisfaction is always tentative and conditional, depending on the outcome. The performance, you see, is just a means to an end - winning. Some folks get so worried about having a good outcome, that they trip up the process.

Process-oriented people are intrinsically motivated. They see great worth in the practice sessions and in the performance itself for enjoyment, learning and growth, regardless of the outcome. They have a strong sense of control and self-determination over their activities. Naturally, they want to succeed or win as much as the next guy, but if they lose they can take it in stride and recoup faster. Winning is just the icing on the cake. Process-oriented people are happier and more willing to give it their all. Even though they may be highly

195

disciplined, they are free to have more fun. This helps them streamline their energy.

EXTRINSIC MOTIVATION - FRIEND OR FOE?

Extrinsic motivation encourages spotty, inconsistent performance. As soon as the pressure, fear, or promise of reward lessens, or the contest is over, performance lessens. Therefore, extrinsic motivators need to be continually renewed or beefed up.

But wait! There's more. Numerous studies have shown that **extrinsic motivation actually blocks and decreases intrinsic motivation**. When subjects come to see themselves as working to get a reward, they are less likely to view that work as interesting in its own right and worth pursuing voluntarily.

Competition had the same effect as offering tangible rewards. Amabile told a group of 7-11 year old girls that those who made the best collages would win prizes, while another group was not asked to compete. The girls trying to beat their peers produced works judged as less creative on several indicators - less spontaneous, complex, and varied. Competition, like other external motivators, stunts creativity.[2] Many other studies over the years have yielded the similar results.

When you take an activity that is an end in itself and make it into a means to an end, not only does interest fluctuate, but performance suffers.

196

You can see how this dimension can impact how we handle projects at work, sports, contests, training, school - you name it. We need to pay more attention to what excites and empowers, or bores and limits people when we set up jobs or educational curricula.

Obviously, no one is going to get rid of external motivators. The question is one of emphasis, where to put your energy. Intrinsic motivation works better, but it is often trickier to develop. It is created by providing personally meaningful challenges and opportunities (flow experiences - Key 5) in an empowering organizational culture (Key 8).

WHERE DO GOALS FIT IN?

Many goals are extrinsic by definition - promotions, money, houses, cars and boats. Nothing is wrong with that. Extrinsic motivators actually work best in situations where intrinsic motivation is lacking. They usually do **not**, as we have seen, create internal motivation. Nor should they be the focus during performance itself.

The most powerful goals are intrinsic ones - goals of growth, knowledge, process of accomplishment, autonomy of action, contribution. Next come extrinsic goals that are personally relevant to you for your and your family's well-being. An often-distant third are extrinsic goals such as helping your team make a sales quota, or boosting your firm's marketshare (unless of course, you own the firm!)

197

"ACHIEVING" HAPPINESS

Happiness is not a condition to be achieved. It is a state to be experienced. As soon as I say I want to strive for "Happiness", I'm admitting that I'm not happy. True happiness-joy-satisfaction befuddle us today. We look for excitement, entertainment, things, or intangibles such as status or power to grant us happiness. Properly used, all of these things are perfectly fine. They can produce fun, enjoyment, occasionally some fulfillment. They just can't make us happy. In fact, striving for them will **destroy our happiness** to the degree that we **depend on them** to bring us happiness!

Likewise happiness is not a just state of ecstasy, bliss, nor can it be found in the Zone. We can all **get** to such a state, but we **can't stay** there. Many folks run from one fun or exciting activity to another, or do drugs, hoping to avoid their inner alienation and lack of fulfillment. But as the old saying goes, "the faster they run, the behinder they get." The more we chase happiness, the more it eludes us.

True happiness does not equal fun.[3] Fun is a bonus of happiness. It is not it's foundation. In fact, happiness occasionally involves pain, hurt, and just plain hard work. We recognize this to some degree in sports and fitness: "no pain, no gain".

198

Consider what enhances **real** happiness - a good marriage, raising children, personal growth, career achievement, sound friendships, religious or spiritual commitment, or civic or charitable work, for example. All of these are fraught with difficulty and hurt from time to time. To **fully live** is to experience both ecstasy and suffering. One can't fully appreciate one without the other, nor can one find lasting happiness by chasing one in order to avoid the other.

True happiness is an inner quality. It's up to me. This makes it unconditional. Once I know this, I know that nothing external can take it away, unless I surrender it. Circumstances may buffet me, possessions and relationships can come and go, but my happiness - joy - satisfaction are mine.

Happiness relates to love, inner peace, and emotional well being. Ego and self-struggle are transcended. Happiness is to live life fully, accepting both pleasure and pain as essential to growth and fulfillment, and being open to all positive possibility.

Mark Epstein, MD, states "Happiness is the ability to receive the pleasant without grasping, and the unpleasant without condemning...we rarely come to terms with the fact that good and bad are two sides of the same coin, that those who make pleasures possible are also the source of our misery...trying to split pleasure and displeasure off from each other only makes us mire deeply in our own dissatisfaction."[4]

Happiness boosts confidence and capability.

Ultimately, **happiness has a mutually enhancing relationship with significance**, with meaning and purpose. Herein The 8 Keys have almost come full circle.

FINAL THOUGHTS

"Activity and reflection should ideally complement and support each other. Action by itself is blind, reflection impotent."

Mihaly Czikszentmihalyi [5]

"To laugh often and much; to win the respect of intelligent people and the affection of children, to earn the appreciation of honest critics and endure the betrayal of false friends; to appreciate beauty, to find the best in others; to leave the world a bit better, whether by a healthy child, a garden patch, or a redeemed social condition; to know that even one life has breathed easier because you have lived. This is to have succeeded."

Ralph Waldo Emerson

Chapter Eighteen

IMPLEMENTING KEY 7 EXERCISES

You have probably noticed, as we are coming full circle on The 8 Keys System and are approaching the home stretch, that different threads and concepts from the preceding Keys are beginning to converge. This is by design.

Growth is not linear, but occurs through the process of revisitation. Each time we revisit a topic or practice, we do so in a slightly different manner, integrating and expanding our growth and outcomes. Several of the practices below function that way.

Also, many of the issues in Key 7 cannot be forced. They can, however, be **shaped** through redirection of attention and energy, and rediscovery.

All this said, let's go.

(1)   **Determine what floats your boat**. Revisit your Keys 1 and 6 priorities lists. Look at your job tasks at work, and the things you do in other venues of life. Which of these activities turn you on, or provide genuine intrinsic interest for you?   Take your job apart.What specific sub-tasks are most engaging for you. Why? Do you see any patterns emerging across different venues such as work, social, family, etc.?

(2)   **Classify your motivators**. List as many things as you can that truly motivate you: money, meaningful work, friendly colleagues, whatever. Then classify them as internal or external. Notice any differences in your performance when your prime drivers are intrinsic and when they're extrinsic? What differences do you notice in quality of output, fun in the process, stress level, excitement Vs. boredom, spirit of your work, feelings, etc. In what endeavors do you find yourself performing as the Artist-Worker?

(3)   **Refuse to wait for Santa Claus. Take action within your area of freedom**. It' so easy to cast responsibility for creating meaningful work onto "management" or some other outside agent. Maybe certain things would function or perform better if restructured. Don't wait for that to happen.

Reinvent your job.   Decide that you are in charge of **how** you do your job, the attitudes you bring to it, and the motives it serves in your life. Re-examine your Area of Freedom, this time in terms of intrinsic motivation and process satisfaction. Regardless of your organizational sphere of influence, you're the boss over what you do. Decide how you will run your area to improve intrinsic motivation. This and the next two exercises help build greater autonomy and self-direction on the job which is crucial to experiencing flow.

(4)   Trade an "I have to" mentality with an "I get to" mentality. Norman Vincent Peale said that so many people

look at their jobs in terms of what they've got to do, rules they must follow, etc   He felt, correctly, that that focus drained energy.   Rather, he suggested that people look at what they "get to do" on their jobs - create, meet new people, produce something of value, or touch lives of people around them.   It bears repeating: how you view your job is up to you, and will determine your satisfaction.

(5)   **Turn your job into a quest**. Use it as a vehicle for making greater things happen: improve teamwork, finding a problem to solve, better customer service, increased skills/knowledge, improved communication, greater variety of activities, etc. Create the "positive stretch". Set challenging personal performance or learning targets based on your personal interests and needs. There's no job that can't have additional meanings and creativity super-imposed upon it. **Invent a challenge, then rise to it**.

Consider the theme of the following Elizabethan folk song:

"Twas on a jolly summer's morn, the 21st of May
Giles Scroggins took his turnip hoe,
with which he trudged away;
'For some delights in hay-makin',
and some they fancies mowin,
But of all the jobs that I likes best,
give I the turnip hoein'.

For the fly, the fly, the fly be on the turnip,
and it be all me eye for I to try to keep fly off
the turnip'." (2)

Scroggins knew how to turn a mundane job into a Zone experience, with, I'm sure, quite a bit of play.

(6)   **Build skills/grow your mind**. Target specific learning goals or skills to develop further. Build on strength. Either target necessary job skills or new skills tangential to your job that will broaden your repertoire. **Cross-Train**. Learn as much as you can about your industry trends beyond the sphere of your own firm's activities. This may put you in a position to guide, suggest, or input new strategy.

(7)   **Goal alignment**. This was also mentioned in Key 6. See how your personal interests, goals and objectives mesh with those of your firm. If you bring them in line or find good links between them, you will more readily be able to identify with your firm's activities. You may find your work more satisfying.

(8)   **Develop your sense of curiosity and wonder**. Ask questions. Get to know the background and the "why's" not just the "what's".

(9)   **Let your "inner child" out to play**. Find ways to bring appropriate fun, humor and levity to the job. Encourage surprise. Take play breaks, run, skip or dance down the hall. Keep a stuffed animal in your office, etc.

(10)   **Find ways to blend "work" and "play"**. In our society, we artificially divorce work from play too completely. Often we have less fun at work because we believe we're **not supposed** to have fun there. For too long, play at work has been discouraged.

Peter Senge states that there are three ways that organizational learning occurs: through teaching, through changing the rules of the game, and through play. Arie DeGeus, head of planning for Royal Dutch/Shell says, "Play is the most rare and potentially the most powerful." (3)

Tom   Peters   suggests   "organizing   around enthusiasms" allowing teams and individuals to do things that interest them or fit with their particular strengths. (4)

Play not only lets off steam, it refreshes and recharges our batteries. It promotes creativity and novel approaches to problems. It also more deeply bonds the people who must work together, building greater common purpose and understanding.

Play opens the door to a more experimental attitude. Research and experience on attitudes and work styles regarding computers yielded interesting results. Older workers see them as "work", while teenagers play with them. Thus, the teens have more fun, learn faster, and are more active and innovative in their use. They often outperform their adult counterparts, using broader applications of computers than adults do. (5)

(11)   **Develop fun in your avocational life**. Develop a new hobby, or take more time to play on a regular basis, just for the fun of it, without any demands for an outcome. Involve friends and family.

(12)   **"Measure" yourself by your own standards** rather than feeling that you must live up to others' or society's standards of success. This is a Key 3 issue but it is also relevant here, for your happiness. If you haven't solved it for yourself yet, it may pay you to revisit it now.

(13)   **Treat yourself lovingly** - physically, nutritionally, emotionally, spiritually, socially. Don't worry about "balancing your life", if balance means giving all major aspects equal time. Balance works for some, but is a disaster for others. Don't sweat it, but make sure that your major needs and aspects such as work, play, social, love, etc. get met to a personally satisfying degree.

(14)   Finally, **infuse daily activities with meaning and purpose**. Revisit your personal definition of significance and your sense of personal mission. Find ways to intertwine meaning and purpose into your daily work and personal life in a manner that works best for you.

AFFIRMATIONS FOR KEY 7
I experience greater meaning and purpose in my life every
     day.
I am happy and content, whatever comes.
I find new enjoyment and benefit in my daily activities.
I do what I love, I love what I do.

I am more motivated and energized every day.
What's worth doing, is worth doing significantly.
I am a person of peace.
I am fun to be around.
I bring joy wherever I go.

VISUALIZATIONS FOR KEY 7

1.   Mentally rehearse yourself as an Artist-Worker. See yourself happily engaged in your work, creating new challenges and experiencing the thrill of mastery.

2.   Visualize yourself as happy and content. Get in touch with the things, persons or events that support your happiness.

FINAL THOUGHTS

"I always figured the way to enjoy life in an impossible situation was just to pretend you owned whatever it was (your company). I'm going to figure out what I would want me to do in my particular job if I owned the company. Then I'll see how close I could come to doing it that way."

"You begin to have fun doing what nobody else is doing. Other people are doing things that they think make them look smart, or make them look special, or may get them something, or cover their ass, and they think they can get away with it." [6]

Robert Townsend

INTRODUCTION TO KEY 8

EXPANSION/OUTREACH

As we begin Key 8, we close the circle. While other people have been involved in the outworking of Keys 1-7, the main emphasis was personal, on you and your development. The first 7 keys have helped to ready you for this one. Master those, and success in Key 8 is much more easy and natural.

We cannot positively engage others unless we ourselves are strong, We cannot love others more than we love ourselves. Only when we have achieved healthy emotional Self-Reliance can we be ready for Interdependence - true give and take in mutually satisfying, caring relationships. **Interdependent people know they both need and can help each other, and that - within reason - both are essential.** As Phil Jackson , coach of the Chicago Bulls, says, "The main thing is to create a community where players identify with and support each other."

Down through the years hundreds of thousands of books have been written on some aspect of relationships from romance novels to self-help. Yet it all boils down to one central crux - the ability to identify with and encourage others as equals with yourself, to help others feel important, powerful, capable, and wanted, and to help them become their best. This is the essence of "empowerment", and healthy relationships in any setting from work to love. It's the cornerstone of Key 8.

No one can be fully successful and happy outside of a loving, caring relationship.

Key 8

"Invest in others <u>before</u> you expect them to invest in you."

Anon

"True power is the ability to endanger voluntary cooperation."

H.A.Olson

"No one cares how much you know, until they know how much you care."

Anon

"Givers gain."

Ivan Misner, Cofounder

"The best form of 'self-help' is to develop the skills of active citizenship."

H.A.Olson

"The vehicle to success and happiness in the next millennium can be summed up in two words: Other people. Drive carefully!"

H.A.Olson

"You alone can do it, but you can't do it alone."

Anon

"The best gift that you can give to others is to honestly and heartily <u>expect them to succeed</u>.

H.A.Olson

Chapter Nineteen

KEY 8 - RELATIONSHIPS
"Empower yourself through empowering others."

"You really spelled 'cat' very well. I've never seen it spelled any better." - teacher to first-grader who only got one word correct on his spelling test.

In that one little example rests all the elements of empowerment. Many people are tired of hearing the "E-word". As a buzzword, we've succeeded in beating it to death, without really grasping how to accomplish it.

It's very simple, really...simple, but not always easy. It's about as easy as thinking up the opening line of this chapter if it were **your** child who "failed" a spelling test!

Empowerment is more a mindset and a relationship than a set of techniques. Once you get the hang of it, however, empowerment becomes very natural. If you've been applying the 8 Keys, you're 7/8ths of the way there.

Real empowerment is seeing in others things they don't yet see in themselves, and helping them to bring those things out, to be fully their best. It means that you fully <u>expect</u> them to succeed.

WHY EMPOWERMENT?

Because no other way works any more. Everywhere, old hierarchical systems of command-and-follow-without-question are collapsing around our ears. Power is being redefined away from vertical, directive, above - below relationships in favor of a more collaborative, horizontal - in fact, **circular**-approach: equals with differing skills and personalities all helping each other. What goes around comes around. When it comes to the path of their destiny, today people don't want to be "led". They want to help navigate.

We're finally beginning to realize at the end of this century what psychiatrist Alfred Adler said near beginning of it: **Mankind is socially embedded.** There is no such thing as total independence. We are all connected. The World Wide Web is much more than a computer term.

Alienation, not drugs, crime, or poverty, is the greatest socioeconomic problem of our age. It lies at the root of many of the rest of our social ills. Yet our society preaches "independence" to a fault. It does its darndest to inhibit the attachment process that began with mother in infancy. Traditional "winning" is meant to separate winners from also-rans. We have mistaken "independence" with "individuation", the process of self-definition and self-development. As a result, our society has become dependence-phobic. As Dr. Karen Walant says, "many people feel that they are prohibited from needing an other, from disintegrating into the arms of another...our society's

213

insistence on autonomy has also encouraged a sense of detachment from our inner thoughts and feelings as well as an inability to form intimate relationships with others..." (1)

The answers lie in **recognizing our true connectedness and discovering how to capitalize upon it to everyone's benefit, without fearing it nor losing ourselves in it**. Let's come down to earth now and start by looking at how we use...

PERSONAL POWER

Power can be both formal and informal. Every relationship is an opportunity to assert personal power vis-à-vis another person. Most of us think of power as a **commodity**, and therefore think of it in terms of scarcity or abundance, and who's got it Vs who doesn't. The truth is, power is possessed by all of us, and is really more of a **process**.

Power today is more relationship-oriented. We operate within a series of linkages between people, which transcends issues of authority, autocracy and autonomy.

The best practical yardstick of personal power in groups is the **ability to create voluntary cooperation**. If one is the "leader", but cannot gain cooperation from "followers", what power does he or she really have? Coercion eventually leads to rebellion or sabotage. Fear no longer works when people stop being afraid.

214

Let's never confuse cooperation with compliance. In the latter, people obey but their hearts aren't in it. True cooperation is heartfelt. People are both **able and willing**.

MOTIVATION

Pressure Power, regardless of how benevolent, is the approach inherent in the old hierarchical structure of bosses and underlings. The main method has been power-over, command and demand. The underlying goal was dominance, and the power base was fear of punishment or the promise or loss of reward. The fundamental motivational question has been "How can I **make** them perform?" Whether through stick or carrot, threats or rewards, the basic power orientation is the same.

This is an impossible question. No one can "make" someone else perform if he refuses to cooperate and is willing to pay the price of resistance. The power to say "no" is irrevocable. It has always been true: government exists by consent of the governed. Power is not the same as "authority", which is ascribed. Power is more natural and spontaneous.

Pressure Power is now giving way to **Presence Power**, the method of positive influence. **The goal is to win people over.** The power base is willing contribution, cooperation and teamwork. The fundamental motivational questions here is "How can I **encourage** them to perform?" We're not talking bribery here. That's a pressure-power tactic! Presence Power honestly and legitimately views people as #1. Encouragement evokes genuine respect, caring, concern and faith in others. It trusts in their loyalty, willingness and desire to perform if their needs are met.

Question is, how do we get there from here?

ENCOURAGEMENT -
THE HEART OF EMPOWERMENT

Positive encouragement can only flourish in a climate of trust and safety. If I'm going to encourage others, they need to know that I'm safe to deal with. Fortunately, trust, safety and encouragement are reciprocal; building one enhances the other two.

Central to encouraging others is recognizing who is in charge of their success. **If I feel personally responsible** for your success, I may push you or pressure you. I may try to force you into my paradigm or time-frame. I may accidentally get in your way or turn you off while trying to help.

If I correctly **see you as responsible for your success**, my role shifts. I am primarily your resource, your cheerleader, perhaps a coach - helping you to determine your own goals and actions in your own way. Good encouragers care, but they also respect their boundaries. They resist temptations to get over- involved or to do for others what they should be doing for themselves. Encouragers respect people's right to self-determination, and honor individual differences in experiences, needs,

216

values and approaches. Of course, within any organization, whether it be a company, family or nation, certain processes and boundaries apply. Freedom must always be balanced with responsibility.

People who are skilled at encouraging others recognize that you can't motivate "groups", only **individuals**. Being a "team" may provide a common goal and mission, but it does not obliterate individuality. Hopefully, **teams capitalize on individual differences**. In fact, you can't "motivate" anyone. All motivation is self-motivation. Your job is to help ring their inner chimes, touch a chord, provide the right conditions so that they turn themselves on.

Losoncy [1] identified five conditions for encouragement:

(1)   **Acceptance** - Being able to value a person just as he or she is, without them having to conform to our preconceptions in order to be viewed as worthwhile.

(2)   **Non-Blaming, Non-Judgmental Attitude** - Blame, put-downs, destructive criticism and punishments must be excluded from your relationship. Fear must be eliminated. Only then can a person be free to open up, share new ideas, take risks or be themselves.

(3)   **Empathy** - The ability to **really listen** to others and to understand the underlying meaning and feelings which accompany their words and actions. Empathy is being able

to put yourself in another's shoes and accurately see a situation from their perspective...and then to communicate that understanding so that the other person knows that you understand.

(4) **Sincere Confidence** that the person is capable of succeeding. There is tremendous power in the expectations we have of others. Others sense our expectations in our looks, words, and actions even if we never openly voice them, and tend to live up or down to them. Knowing that someone has faith in you is a potent motivator. Set high but reachable standards. Then do everything in your power to help them meet them.

(5) **Enthusiasm** - Being able to openly and genuinely express your feelings of appreciation, excitement or pleasure when someone has taken a risk, attempted something new, or met a goal. Success is not essential; **effort** is. Encouragers are good cheerleaders for their people. They don't just believe in them; they root for them.

Positive encouragement communicates loud and clear that **you respect and value people for themselves, not just for their outcomes** or their use to you. It makes people feel wanted and important in their own right; that they are an integral part and that the organization wouldn't be the same without them.

ENCOURAGEMENT VS. PRAISE

We often confuse the two but they are really quite different. Ever notice how people sometimes get uncomfortable when we give them compliments? Part of the problem may lie in the nature of praise.

First of all, praise is a **reward**. It comes after the fact. This makes it a **judgment**, an **evaluation**, an **outcome**, just like criticism. Praise is something I have to earn, so it makes my value conditional. I'm OK enough **if** I did a good enough job or met your expectations.

Second, people often praise one's native talents or abilities. "Good girl", "You're so smart", etc. While this is natural, it is not as effective. It can actually be embarrassing and demotivating.

Encouragement occurs at the beginning and throughout the process. It shows interest and faith in the person which is independent of the outcome. For example, take a comedy act. Praise is complimenting the comedian afterward, while encouragement is listening, smiling and laughing at his jokes.

WHAT TO ENCOURAGE?

When you encourage, focus on the behavior, not the person. Telling a coworker, "You really have a good grasp on this material," or "I'm pleased that you accomplished that so quickly", is much more effective than saying "You're so smart."

219

Behavior-focus is particularly important when one fails or the performance is sub-par. People often know when they goof up. Inside they may already feel stupid. The potential for shame is high. Making them feel foolish now or ridiculing them will only risk shutting down their efforts in the future.

Don't ignore or whitewash poor performance, but focus on the positive effort put forth: "I'm sorry this project didn't turn out as well as you expected. I'm sure you're disappointed (empathy). You put real effort and creative energy into it and I appreciate that. Let's see how we can get it back on track. Is there any way I can help or is there anything else you need?"

Behavior-focused vs. person-focused praise has shown fascinating results. Dweck and Mueller told fifth-graders who did a set of math problems that they "must have worked hard", "must be smart" or just that they "did well". Next, the kids completed another problem set and were all told they "did a lot worse."

The "hardworking" children were much more likely to take problems home for extra practice, to say that they enjoyed the tasks, and to out-perform the "smart" ones on later tasks.

The children praised for their natural abilities were less resilient. Their performance and motivation suffered after their "failure", and they tended to inflate their scores when reporting them to others. Again, this kind of praise makes worth conditional, and shifts the task from an end in itself (Key 7) to a means to an end, i.e. a way to work for a pat on the back. These kids began to measure their worth by their test results (Aha! the Triple Error again, set up in this situation by "praise".)

Dweck states, "The kind of praise that all of society thinks is wonderful...makes kids very vulnerable. Parents need to focus on what children put into a task, rather than make implications about the worth of the child." [3]

Think that this applies only to kids, that we strong, capable adults have outgrown such susceptibility? Guess again!

Bottom line: Remember Will and Imagination? **Humans are extremely suggestible**. We draw subconscious conclusions about the experiences and reactions that affect us, which can instantly alter our self image. That why shame can be so devastating. That's also why positive encouragement can be so powerfully liberating.

CREATING TRUST

Trust is the most critical component for peak performance in teams and organizations. Where it is lacking, people always hold back.

Today the key to competitive advantage lies in the"3-I's" - Intelligence, Information, Ideas. Above most other skills, people's Creativity - their use of the three I's -

221

is particularly sensitive and responsive to the presence or absence of trust and encouragement. High trust and encouragement enable it to flourish.

While fear and shame can shoot through the roof instantly, trust and faith take time to build. That's why it's so important to be consistent and "walk the talk" with the people you work and live with. Be careful that in your daily actions you're not giving with one hand while taking away with the other.

Motivational theorist, Fred Hertzberg, studied the major world religions to see what made them successful over thousands of years. He found ten characteristics they all have in common. Each religion provides their adherents continuity, emotional support, belonging and connectedness (being part of the team), solace/comfort, an outlet for our altruistic needs, a sense of the cosmic (connection with a power greater than ourselves - which could also equate to an overriding cause or purpose), a source of good feelings, experience of growth, assurance, and a sense of self-confidence and self-worth. [4]

Organizations that have drawn and energized billions of people over the history of mankind must be doing something right! While none of these factors are panaceas, nor are always done perfectly, in combination they create a potent climate for trust, support and growth. Applying these factors both personally and organizationally can reap powerful dividends. To quote another religious teacher, "Go thou and do likewise."

FINAL THOUGHTS

Your greatest power resides in gentleness:

- You have no enemies unless you think you do; then you will create enemies. Be proactively defenseless.
- When you don't need to defend yourself, you are free to act.
- Gentleness is irresistible. Think back again to the persons who were most positively meaningful and influential in **your** life. How did they treat you? Did they demonstrate the 5 conditions of encouragement?
- Caring requires daring.
- Gentleness is having the power **not** to react when everything within you says you should.

"Whoever would be first among you must first become your servant."

Jesus of Nazareth

As the "Enlightened One" and his disciples were sitting around a campfire, he asked them, "How do you know when night is over and day has begun?" The disciples debated for hours and could not reach agreement. Finally the "Enlightened One" said, "Here is my answer: when one looks into the eyes of another person and sees a brother or a sister."

Reverend Ronald Nelson

Chapter Twenty

IMPLEMENTING KEY 8 EXERCISES

By now you've noticed that Key 8 is also about **leadership and coaching skills**. Actually, it's about good people skills, which, by definition, are the heart of good leadership. Regardless of your formal position, good people and leadership skills are critical for **anyone** who wants to be highly successful and happy in the network world of the next Millennium.

This chapter is a catalog of one-to-one empowerment practices and methods. Most of this will sound like common sense. It's actually **uncommon sense**: We know it when we see it, but rarely do we do it **systematically**. Some practices you may have already developed well, while others you may not have considered yet. Some may be appropriate in your varied work and life roles, some may not. As you read through them, think in terms of what you would need to focus upon and develop to become a **world-class encourager**. In so doing, you'll also become a good coach. Create your own specific action plan and follow it, choosing and pacing these practices as you see fit.

Your task is to help others to realize their potential and succeed. This is Key 1 on a personal level. Here's how. You might rate your style on the list below to how much of each practice you're currently doing from 0 to 10. 0 = never and 10 = almost always

(1)   **See yourself as a change agent for good**. Accept that role fully and willingly. You are fully qualified to make a difference in peoples' lives. You do anyway, whether you think about it or not. How much more impact can you have if you do it by design. So many people say, "Who me?" Yes, you. You don't have to be Mother Theresa. We're talking about strengthening your daily style of interaction.

(2)   **Think "mutuality"**. Train your mind to recognize your connectedness. Think the web, the network. When you make an important decision or action, consider what kind of interpersonal impact it will make. After all, we're all in the same boat.

(3)   **Demonstrate the power of your own integrity and self-respect**. Be consistent and honest. Decide what your core values are and never compromise them. You need to be flexible and open to influence on many lesser things. That's OK as long as you hold fast to what you are and believe.

(4)   **Demonstrate the power of love, not just the love of power**. [1] As said so many times before, this is where your real power lies.

(5)   **Show faith in others' inner resources** and capabilities, and their willingness to learn and grow. Often when others resist participation, the problem lies in how or

for what tasks they are approached. Yet we rarely question that when resistance occurs. Rather, we look at the resistance as "not being a team player" or being oppositional.

(6)   **Promote experimentation, creativity and honest debate**. Draw out new ideas, stimulate discussion. Don't insist on total agreement. Well-meaning debate can push creativity forward.

(7)   **Celebrate mistakes**. No one will succeed who is afraid to fail. The Wright Brothers made over 1000 "failed" test flights before their airplane finally flew. Where would we be if inventors felt they **had** to do it right the first time? Focus on effort made, and look toward how to improve the next time.

(8)   **Be present and visible**, especially if you're a leader. If you're truly an encourager, others will see it as support, not spying.

(9)   **Catch people doing well**. Be a goodness detective. Without overdoing it, publicly comment on positive performance **as it is occurring.** Don't wait for the outcome. Use Igniter Phrases (Appendix 3). People need to know that their **efforts** are appreciated, not just their results. Let your times of recognition always exceed your times of reproof.

(10)   **Show your appreciation. Be lavish with recognition,** both public and private. John was V.P. of sales for a midsize firm. He always wrote his peoples'

227

accomplishments up in the company newsletter. When asked why, he said, "My people make me possible."

(11)　**Share credit wherever you can**. Remember Lao Tsu's leadership quote from Key 2, "and because he takes no credit, credit never leaves him.."

(12)　**Ask for help or input, even when you don't need it**. This may be the ultimate Key 2 test, especially for us guys. This makes others feel important. Everyone wants a chance to help out and feel they are being relied upon. If someone offers an unsolicited good idea, say, "Great thought. I appreciate it", not "Yeah, I already thought of it."

(13)　**Share useful information widely and wisely**. Obviously some information is proprietary and confidential. Yet most people are more closed-mouthed than they need to be. People want to be kept in the loop. When you share. you show trust.

(14)　**Share your power**. That's how you gain power.

(15)　**Take interest in other people's private lives** such as interests, hobbies, family. Don't be nosy, however, and never betray a confidence.

(16)　**Honor and promote diversity**. Learn to understand how different gender, ethnic and racial backgrounds affect people's experiences, attitudes and beliefs. See diversity as a rich tapestry. Get past your biases. America is no longer an homogenized melting pot but a thick stew, with each piece identifiable, contributing to the overall taste and nourishment. Never forget that at the core of humanness, we're more alike than different. Regardless of expression, we all have the same fundamental needs.

(17) **Let others be themselves,** OK in their own right. They don't need to conform to your will and desires to prove their worth.

(18) **Hold people accountable for results, not processes.** Within proper ethical, fiscal and time parameters let people solve problems their own way. Don't micromanage. Keep abreast of their activity, give them the resources they need to succeed, then keep out of the way.

(19) **Accept no excuses.** Be fair. True emergencies will arise, yet to routinely accept others' excuses is actually demotivating and shows others that you don't really care or don't expect high performance.

(20) **Set high and crystal clear expectations,** but not unreasonable ones. Create the "positive stretch". Highly motivated people will love the challenge. **Keep your expectations for each person in line with what you know he or she is able to do.** Discouraged or underperforming people will need more of a helping hand than a critical lecture.

(21) **Confront problems head on.** Don't deny them or sweep them under the rug. Don't be punitive or demeaning. Focus on creating positive solutions. Use problems as

opportunities for further growth and development. Be very careful not to lapse into judging, self-righteousness, "I'm OK, you're not OK" morally superior, or veiled aggressive attitudes, words, or actions.

(22)   **Communicate your feelings**, again, honestly, but with diplomacy and tact. Mr. Rogers said "feelings that are mentionable   are   manageable".   Sharing   feelings demonstrates trust. It's the emotions that you won't or feel you can't talk about that get you. When others can see that you can "clear the air" and that they won't get hurt, they can feel safe. Others stay on edge if they suspect that you have feelings which you're not sharing.

(23)   **Listen carefully, attentively, empathically**. Hear people out and **listen for their feelings and perceptions that underlie their words**. When unsure of their meaning, ask for clarification. Don't interrupt, jump in, or instantly criticize an unfeasible idea. In your response, let the person know you've heard his feelings: "You're excited about getting the Smith contract", or "Sounds like you're really angry about what Bill said to you." The feeling vocabulary (Appendix 2) can help you here. People often express feelings in vocal tone, facial expression, body language etc. Often they don't label them directly, yet their feelings are important to them. Reflecting back to them how you perceive they're feeling is a very powerful trust-builder. It shows you care and because so few people bother to do it, You'll really score points even if you guess wrong.

(24)   **Use "I" messages, not You-messages** when you want to share a concern. A You-message is "You really blew it." or "How could you be so ...!" These make people feel bad, defensive, and often angry. They promote resistance.

I-messages tell someone how **you** feel. The focus is on you, not them. The formula is

a.	I feel _____ (feeling)_____
b.	When (non judgmental statement of behavior)
c.	Because (concrete, tangible impact on you)

Item (b) reduces defensiveness. Item (c) is critical because it brings reason into the discussion and shows the other person a legitimate cause for your feelings. **Most people want to help**. If you show them how you're affected, they are usually more willing to change.

Here's an example: (a) "I'm worried (b) because you missed the Smith contract deadline. (c) Now our backs are to the wall on delivery and we might lose their business." Next steps: await his or her response and deal with that, then shift to problem-solving mode: "How can we repair the situation?" and use your Key 4 skills.

Remember, most people spout off when they're upset because they're frustrated and don't know what else to do. I-messages are a trust-building alternative. Practice the formula when you're calm, so that you can use it naturally when you're upset.

(25)   **Recognize people's claims to fame** [2] Everyone has at least several claims to fame - skills or talents that they do very well, or high points in their lives, which make their feelings soar. When they talk about it, they light up. Enthusiasm reigns. If no one else cares, however, people may become apathetic about those skills or high points and devalue their importance. By showing interest, however, you validate others' feelings of worth and importance.

(26)   **Be considerate and kind to those in difficulty.** Do so quietly, without publicity or fanfare.

(27)   **Mentor, coach or train someone else.** Help and encouragement are the coin of the realm. They're made to go around. Chet Atkins helped country singer Suzy Bogguss get her start and mentored her along the way. Why? "A couple of guys helped me out an awful lot, and without them I don't know where I'd be. Probably dead. Helping people. That's the way we pay back." [3]

Key 8 - it's what you do with Keys 1-7.

AFFIRMATIONS FOR KEY 8

I'm a world-class encourager.
I build bridges.
I bring out the best in everyone I meet.
I'm a winner when I make others winners.
Everyone I meet is my teacher.
Everyone I meet is a hidden treasure.
I see the best in everyone.
I'm cool, calm and fair.
(You might create affirmations about areas you wish to develop further.)

VISUALIZATIONS FOR KEY 8

1. Mentally rehearse yourself handling a difficult interpersonal situation with optimism, caring and encouragement. See yourself keeping your cool and making it come out well.

2. Visualize yourself in situations where you're coaching, helping, teaching, or mentoring others. See yourself being comfortable and effective, making an impact. See that person succeed because you helped. Feel personal feelings of satisfaction and accomplishment.

FINAL THOUGHTS

- Real power is when they think about you when you're absent. What do you want them thinking?

- Unity is truth, division is falsehood.

- There is no such thing as a "personal problem". All problems are social, having interpersonal impact.

- **Where you don't find love, put it. Then you will find it.**

Hug o' War

I will not play at Tug o'war
I'd rather play at Hug o'war
Where everyone hugs
Instead of tugs,
Where everyone giggles
And rolls on the rug,
Where everyone kisses,
And everyone grins.
And everyone cuddles
And everyone wins.

Shel Silverstein [4]

234

EPILOGUE

Now you've come full circle.

Where to from here? Onward and upward to Key 1. Growth always is ongoing. There's always more to learn and more fun to have.

If this little Handbook has given you one new idea, boosted you one notch, or brought you one step closer to your goals, it has been worth the time and energy to write and publish it. Regardless, I'd also love to hear from you.

Rudolf Dreikurs, M.D. said,
**"Wherever we are, we are part of the group,
part of the scene, and participate in the shaping of
destiny."**

Thoreau said,

**"Go confidently
in the direction
of your dreams . . .
live the life
you have
imagined."**

CARPE DIEM - SEIZE THE DAY!

235

Appendix I

HOW TO CREATE AFFIRMATIONS AND VISUALIZATIONS

You want a new reality? You start by creating new thoughts and images. By so doing you "reprogram" your subconscious mind to direct thought, feeling and action in such a way as to bring it naturally into existence, without struggle on your part.

Visual imagery combined with positive verbal affirmations, or "self-talk," is the most potent tool for behavior change and growth when conscientiously and consistently used.

Affirmations are positive powerful statements that you repeat to yourself several times a day, perhaps while in front of the mirror in the morning, in your car, at the office. Some people write them out daily, others post them on 3x5 cards where they can read them. Some repeat them to themselves while in a state of relaxation, meditation or self hypnosis. Some do all of these approaches. The point is to flood those ideas into your mind daily to reshape your subconscious programming and your self-image. Work with no more than six or seven affirmations at a time, focused on one or two goals or issues of your choice. Wait to see some results before shifting to another goal. Choose whatever approach suits you best and be consistent and persistent in doing it.

237

There are six "Ps" to effective affirmation construction. Make your affirmations:

(1)　**Personal** - Talk strictly about yourself. Don't use comparisons or competitiveness. For example, don't say, "I beat so-and-so in the sales contest". Rather, "I close ___ sales this month".

(2)　**Positive** - Don't use negative words or any statement that contains "no" or "not"; e.g., say, "I am confident" VS. "I'm not afraid".

(3)　**Powerful** - Use powerful, emotionally charged and motivating language, or words that are particularly meaningful for you, that will evoke positive imagery.

(4)　**Possible** - Frame a statement which is within the range of your capability, but beyond your current performance level.

(5)　**Present Tense** - Make your affirmations in the here and now, not future; e.g., say, "I act", not "I *will* act".

(6)　**Precise** - When applied to goals, affirmations should be as specific as possible; e.g., say "I earn $60,000 this year", rather than "I am financially successful". More general affirmations such as "I am a person of total honor", work well with general behavioral qualities.

Then visualize yourself experiencing or acting out your affirmations.

Visualizations are mental pictures or images. Some people can create a mental mural or movies in their heads, while others may just see colors or fragments of images. That's OK. If you can **imagine** it, that's fine. Although with practice, visualization skill improves.

Visualizations can be done anytime, anywhere, and take only a few seconds to accomplish. However, if you also do your visualizations and affirmations in a relaxed state, it helps to more deeply embed them into your subconscious. This enhances their effectiveness because in the relaxed state, your subconscious mind is more easily accessed and programmed.

Do them in a relaxed state twice a day, such as early morning and at night. Close your eyes, take a few slow deep breaths. Perhaps put on quiet, meditative music if you wish. Count slowly backwards from 10 to 1 to help aid relaxing and then begin your visualizations. Let all of your senses get involved lf you can· sight, sound, smell, touch, taste and feelings.

The six "Ps" apply to visualizations as well. Here are some additional guidelines:

(1)   **See yourself as totally capable**. Trust your creative subconscious to come up with words and pictures in your imagery that will demonstrate your capability; e.g., if visualizing yourself asking for a raise, don't worry first what to say. Let your creative mind provide its ideas as you visualize. In subsequent visualizations you can rehearse these words.

239

(2)   **Pay attention to feelings and physical sensations** which may accompany your imagery. Though often subtle, these may be vital messages which could affect your decisions and success.

(3)   **Be experimental.** Play with various approaches or strategies for your situation. In your mind, see which ones are more comfortable.

(4)   **When visualizing a goal, see yourself as having achieved it** and enjoying its benefits.

(5)   **Use powerful symbolic imagery** as well as realistic imagery. Perhaps see yourself as an eagle soaring free, a dove bringing peace, St. George slaying a dragon, or whatever fits your needs. Have fun with this.

Affirmations and visualizations are included for each Key. Because every reader's situation is different, the affirmations are, of necessity, more general in wording. Create and include some highly specific ones for each Key that fit you specifically. Likewise, you may wish to alter the visualizations. Find what works best for you and practice it daily.

Appendix 2

LIST OF FEELINGS THAT PERSONS HAVE BUT OFTEN FAIL TO IDENTIFY

abandoned	challenged	disappointed	frantic
accepted	charmed	discontented	frightened
adequate	cheated	distracted	frustrated
adamant	cheerful	distraught	free
affectionate	childish	disturbed	full
agony	clever	dominated	fury
almighty	combative	divided	forgiving
afraid	competent	dubious	friendly
ambivalent	competitive	distrustful	
angry	concerned		glad
annoyed	condemned	eager	good
anxious	confused	ecstatic	goofy
apathetic	conspicuous	electrified	gratified
ashamed	contented	empty	greedy
astounded	contrite	embarrassed	grief
awed	cruel	enchanted	groovy
	crushed	energetic	guilty
bad	curious	enervated	gullible
beautiful		enjoy	guilty
betrayed	deceitful	envious	
bitter	defeated	excited	happy
blissful	delighted	evil	hate
bold	dejected	exasperated	heavenly
bored	desirous	exhausted	helpful
brave	despair		helpless
burdened	destructive	fascinated	high
	determined	faunting	homesick
calm	different	fearful	honored
capable	diffident	flustered	horrible
captivated	diminished	foolish	horrified

241

hurt

hysterical

hopeless

humiliated

ignored

immortal

imposed upon

impressed

inhibited

insecure

inferior

inadequate

infatuated

infuriated

inspired

intimidated

isolated

jealous

joyous

jumpy

kicky

kind

keen

laconic

lazy

lecherous

left out

licentious

lonely

longing

loving (love)

low

lustful

mad

maudlin

mean

melancholy

miserable

mystical

misunderstood

naughty

needy

nervous

nice

nutty

obnoxious

obsessed

old

opposed

outraged

overwhelmed

pain

panicked

parsimonious

passionate

peaceful

persecuted

petrified

pity

pleasant

pleased

precarious

pressured

pretty

prim

prissy

proud

quarrelsome

queer

rage

rupture

refreshed

rejected

relaxed

relieved

remorse

resentful

restless

reverent

rewarded

righteous

sad

safe

satisfied

scared

screwed up

servile

settled

sexy

shocked

silly

skeptical

sneaky

solemn

sorrowful

special

spiteful

startled

stingy

strange

stuffed

stupid

stuffed
stupid
stunned
stupefied
suffering
sure
sympathetic

talkative
tempted
tenacious
tender
tense
tenuous
tentative
terrible
terrified

thankful
threatened
thrilled
thwarted
ired
trapped
trusted
troubled

ugly
unappreciated
uneasy
unsettled
used
useless

violent
vehement
vital/vitality
vulnerable
vivacious

warm
weepy
wicked
wonderful
worn-out
worry (ied)
worthwhile

youthful

zany

Appendix 3

IGNITER PHRASES

How you express yourself can boost or kill enthusiasm. Here are some examples of turn-ons and turn-offs.

Phrases That Build People and Get Things Started

I agree!
done.
I looked at this last night and
really liked it!
Let's get right on it.
Good job!
I made a mistake. I'm sorry.
Let's go!
Go ahead...try it.
I like that!
Things are beginning to pop!
I couldn't do that well myself.
That's a great idea.
There's been some good thinking.
I'm glad you brought that up.
That's an interesting idea.
Good work!
I'm very pleased with what
you've done.
You can do it!
You're in high gear.
That's the first time I've had
anyone think of that.
I have faith in you.
Fantastic !

I appreciate what you have

See, you can do it!

That's good!
Let's start a new trend.
Great!
I know it will work.
That's interesting.
Good for you!
I never thought of that.
Congratulations!
Keep going!
Very good!
You're beautiful!
Do that again.
You're right on track.
That's fine!

That's a winner!
We can always depend on you.
We can do a lot with that idea.

Keep up the good work.

244

KILLER PHRASES

How To Destroy Ideas and Chloroform Creative Thinking

A swell idea, but . . .
We've never done it that way.
suggested it

It won't work . . .
We haven't the time.
It's not in the budget.
time.
Too expensive . . .
problem.
We've tried that before
Not ready for it yet.

Too academic . . .
Too hard to administer,
Too much paperwork
Too early . . .

It's not good enough.
There are better ways than that.
It's against our policy.
Who do you think you are?
You haven't considered . . .
being.
It needs more study.
Don't be ridiculous.

Let's not step on their toes.
Somebody would have

before if it were any good.
Too modern . . .
Too old-fashioned . . .
Let's discuss it at some other

You don't understand our

Why start anything now?
All right in theory, but can you
put it into practice?
We have too many projects now.
What you are really saying is . . .
Has anyone else ever tried it?
It has been the same for twenty
years so it must be good.
Let me add to that . . .
I just know it won't work.
Let's be practical.
Let's form a committee.
Let's shelve it for the time

It doesn't fit our program.
Let's get back to reality.

(My apologies to the author. I did not create this list and have no idea who the author is. If I find out, I will credit him or her in the next edition.)

Appendix 4

SHAME - SHAM

The fear of shame is the world's greatest killer of peak performance. We will avoid shame at almost any cost because it is the one emotion that can shatter our confidence and lead us to feel generally incompetent. It shoots holes in our self-image and tarnishes our self-esteem.

What shame creates is a **sham**. Until you understand the **psychobiology** of shame, however, you can never clearly discover the flaws in the brain's logic and learn how to overcome them.

Shame is an emotion that occurs in response to specific stimuli. It is **neurologically programmed and ingrained**. It is part of the brain's wiring. It occurs pretty much the same way in everyone regardless of race or gender, even though intensity and expression may vary from person to person and occasion to occasion.

FALLOUT OF SHAME

When shame hits, it upsets all mental functioning. It renders us incompetent to perform creative and intentional activity. It produces a heightened painful self-awareness in which we are forced to remember our failures. It undercuts every pleasant way we know ourselves, leaving us feeling more foolish, incompetent, or worthless than we felt before the feeling of shame occurred. [1]

We experience a lingering self-doubt and a mighty tendency to avoid putting ourselves into similar situations again. In short, shame makes us gun-shy. As Mark Twain said, "Once a cat sits on a hot stove, it will never do so again. It won't sit on a cold stove either."

Shame, like any other fear, is an **overgeneralization with a failure to discriminate**. If we felt mortified when we were laughed at while giving a speech in elementary school, we might feel panicky about addressing a group fifty years later, even though the circumstances are totally different. But shame blocks logic. Our brain does that to protect us, to keep us out of perceived danger.

THE SHAME-SHOCK PROCESS

Here's how shame works:

- You express yourself or try something new. Or maybe you're just minding your own business.
- You fail, or others make fun, or criticize, or abuse you.
- Good feelings are instantly interrupted. You feel **humiliated**. This triggers specific physical processes: your face flushes, eyes squint and mouth grimaces. Heart rate speeds up. Perhaps you feel an obnoxious feeling in your stomach. You perspire and tense up.
- The brain goes into **cognitive shock**: you can't think clearly, your mind goes blank, you feel like you've forgotten all you knew. Perhaps you stumble for words. Your **working memory** temporarily shuts down.
- The brain begins to scan your memory for past experiences of failure. It scans every area and aspect and period of your life. Naturally, it finds an abundance of past goof-ups. Emotionally, this is what creates the **generalized** feeling of incompetence.
- The immediate pain wears off, but the memory remains, along with greater self-doubt and hesitancy.

• At the moment or in the future, our typical
responses to shame are re-active: avoidance and
denial (from cover-up to drugs), withdrawal (from
silence to hiding to depression), attacking others
(from put-downs to violence), or attacking ourselves
(from deference to masochism).[2] Our egos get
hooked and we become defensive. Ultimately, these
behaviors make matters worse and create greater
potential for more shame.

FOREWARNED IS FOREARMED

If you understand how shame works, you can begin
to recognize the falsity of the self-depreciation conclusions
that you experience. It becomes easier to keep a healthy
self-perspective, to let go of the sense of incompetence and
to challenge self-limiting beliefs, countering them with
examples of past success. If you know, for instance, that
shame temporarily shuts down working memory, you can
more easily resist the idea that you've forgotten all you
knew. You can know that you are not really diminished in
the slightest, even though shame may make you think you
are. Then you are better prepared to take effective action.

Additional Resources

THE PLAYBOOK

The perfect companion to this **Handbook,** the **Playbook** is a write-in tool. It presents all of the **Handbook** exercises, plus more, along with charts and quizzes. It provides space to record your thoughts, actions, progress and results. Those who enjoy journaling will also like using the **Playbook.**

The **Handbook + Playbook** is the perfect tool-kit for self-help and for 8 Keys study and training groups.

THE NEW WAY TO COMPETE
(3rd printing)

Reviewed by Success Magazine as "one of the best selections to help you succeed", this updated edition is filled with strategies to help you cope ethically with competition, and to protect and advance your career. This book is vital for career changers and those working in highly competitive industries or organizations.

Both of the above are available from Insight Publishing Company. Also additional resources are continually in progress. Don't miss out. Contact us today to get on our mailing list.

THE 8 KEYS TRAINING PROGRAMS

If you enjoyed the handbook, you will love **The 8 Keys Training Programs**. They explore each Key in depth and focus on personal breakthroughs and skill building, especially in mental training. We offer several formats from in-house training to executive retreats in a resort setting, to public seminars. All corporate programs are customized to your organization's specific needs. Contact Maximum Potential for details.

Maximum Potential, Inc.
410-581-0817

REFERENCES

Chapter 4
1. Pines, M. Psychological Hardiness. Psychology Today. December 1980, 34-35.

Chapter 5
1. Kawasaki, G. quoted in Adam, M. What a Guy. Performance Strageties. March 1996, 19.
2. Eger, Edith. Personal communication
3. Chanel, C. quoted in Schiller, D. The Little Zen Companion. N.Y. Workman. 1994, 272.
4. Austin, C. Interview on NBC Olympic coverage. 7-29-96.

Chapter 9
1. Viorst, J. The whole truth. How Did I Get To Be 40 and Other Antrocities. N.Y. Simon & Shuster. 1973, 21.

Chapter 10
1. Beecher W., & Beecher, M. Beyond Success and Failure. N.Y. Julian, 1966.

Chapter 11
1. Cultivate your optimism. Executive Strategies Newsletter. April, 1974, 4.
2. Reeve, C. quoted in Carter, B. Are you in control, New Woman. June, 1996, 30.
3. Barfield, C. Interviewed on CBS This Morning, August 12, 1996.
4. Beecher, W.& Beecher, M. Beyond Success & Failure. N.Y. Julian, 1966, 233.

Chapter 12
1. Seligman, M. Learned Optimism. New York: Knoff, 1991.

2. Pilzer, P.Z. Unlimited Wealth: The Theory & Practice of Economic Alcheny. Quoted by Wallace, D. in "Unlimited wealth" Success. June, 1991, 47.

Chapter 13
1. Czikszentmihalyi, M. Flow: The Psychology of Optimal Experience. N.Y. Harper & Row. 1990.

Chapter 14
1. Erickson, D. How to handle a great accomplishment. Shooting Sports USA. December, 1989, 7.

Chapter 15
1. Enos, B. Action shooting with Brian Enos. Shooting Sports USA. (Date unknown.)
2. Tutko, T. & Tosi, U. Sports Psyching. LA. J. P. Tarcher/St. Martins. 1976, 135.
3. Creativity head trips. Psychology Today. Nov.-Dec. 1995, 12.
4. Chopra, D. quoted in Cohen, S. Miracle alert. New Woman. March 1996, 152.
5. IBID 87.

Chapter 16
1. Bassham, L. With Winning In Mind. San Antonio. X-Press, 1988.

Chapter 17
1. Kohn, A. Art for art's sake. Psychology Today. 1987, 52.
2. IBID 54.
3. Prager, D. What makes a happy person? Redbook. 2, 2989, 76, 78.
4. Epstein, M. Opening up to happiness. Psychology Today. 1995, 42, 46.
5. Czikszentmihalyi, M. Flow. The Psychology of Optimal Experience. N.Y. Harper & Row, 1990, 226.

Chapter 18
1.   Blanchard, K. Positive Thinkers get positive results,
        Executive Edge 25. March, 1994, 1.
2.   Turmut Hoein, from Runge, J. Early English Lute
        Songs. New York, Hargail Music Press.
3.   Berg, D. The power of a playful spirit at work.
        Journal For Quality & Participation. July/August 1995, 34.
4.   IBID. 34.
5.   Weil, E. The future is younger than you think.
        Fast Company April/May 1997, 102.
6.   Towsend, R. How to motivate yourself - and more.
        Executive Edge 25, 12, Dec. 1994, 12.

Introduction to Key 8
1.   Simon, R. Systems therapy NBA style.
        Family Therapy Networker March/April 1997, 52.

Chapter 19
1.   Walant, K. An interview with Dr. Karen B. Walant.
        Psychotherapy Book News.
2.   Losoncy, L. Turning People On. Englewood Cliffs:
        Prentice-Hall/Spectrum 1977, 87ff.
3,   Chatterjee, C. Praising your child: what works.
        Psychology Today Sept/Oct 1997, 22.
4.   Shea, G. Company Loyalty: Earning It, Keeping It.
        New York: American Management Association
        1987, 71.

Chapter 20
1.   Intner, R. The NASAP Newsletter 30, 6. August 1997.
2.   Losoncy, L. Turning People On. Englewood Cliffs:
        Prentice-Hall/Spectrum 1977, 111-112.
3.   Atkins, C. & Dowling, C. G. quoted in LIFE. Dec. 1996, 65.
4.   Silverstein, S. Where The Sidewalk Ends. N.Y. Harper,
        1974.

Appendix 4

1, 2.   Nathanson, D. Shame & Pride: Affect, Sex, and the Birth of the Self. New York. Norton, 1992. p. 211, 312ff.

ABOUT THE AUTHOR

Harry A. Olson, Ph.D. is a Maker of Champions. He is internationally recognized as a psychologist, organizational consultant and peak performance and competition coach with over 25 years of daily experience working with top achievers in business, sales and sports. Harry authored four books and several audiocassette albums. He has provided training and consultation for such firms as Berol Chemical & Observera Gray Advertising (Sweden), J.C. Penney, Pfizer, National Institutes of Health and Aberdeen Proving Ground.

You can contact us on the Internet at www.harryolson.com